Let's Take a Trip!

Donald Korach

All rights reserved. No portion of this book may be reproduced, stored in a retrieval system, or transmitted in any form or by any means—electronic, mechanical, photocopy, recording, or other—except for brief quotations in printed reviews, without the prior permission of the author and/or publisher.

Unless otherwise indicated, Scripture quotations used in this book are from the Holy Bible, King James Version.

Copyright © 2015

ISBN-13: 978-1518612756
ISBN-10: 151861275X

Please contact the author at:

Dr. Donald M. Korach, Missionary
(506) 88214944 cell/whatsapp
Email: dkorach@femutua.org

Fe Mutua - Mutual Faith Costa Rica
Phone: (506) 2235-7707
Apdo Postal: 1211-2150, Moravia, San José, Costa Rica.
Email: dkorach@mutualfaith.org
Website:www.femutua.org

Dedication

A special dedication to my family

Marjorie, you make missions, ministry and life possible. You hold the family together and make sure I have a secure place to be just me. Thank you, My Love.

Rachel, you make missions fun. Thanks for reminding me and calling me by my greatest and highest calling. In the ministry people call me Doctor, Pastor, Missionary and sometimes even Apostle, but thank you for calling me Dad.

Donnie, just as your sister you make missions and the ministry fun. You step up and help anywhere possible. You are my fearless one, and I commend you for making me braver than I really am.

Don and Sandy Korach, Mom and Dad, you have been with me since the very beginning. You supported me when we didn't even know what it was to be a missionary. You truly are great people of Faith, Hope and Love.

Special Thanks

As Missionaries, we can truly do nothing by ourselves. We need others to support us financially. We need others to help train us in foreign cultures. We need pastors to allow us to minister in their churches and assist us in touching the lives of their people.

Special thanks to my supporters. You make ministry possible. You touch lives every day.

Special thanks to Keith Hershey for giving me a ministry home to express missions.

Special thanks to all those who contributed "A word..." to this project. You are a witness to what the Lord has done over these last thirty years.

Special thanks to Virginia Real. You arrived in Costa Rica just in time to help with *"Let's take a Trip"* and push it past the grammatical finish line.

Special thanks to Angi Payne Sutton. You were the first to say *"Of course you can write a book!"* Now, thanks to your editing it is a reality.

"Lets take a Trip!"

Don Korach
Missionary
Mutual Faith, Costa Rica
dkorach@femutua.org
dkorach@mutualfaith.org

Table of Contents

Day 1 – Page 1
Blessed Coming In and Going Out- It's a Blessing Day!

Day 2 – Page 17
A Day for Ladies Only Ministry!

Day 3 – Page 29
Everyone is Here – Let the Fun begin!

Day 4 – Page 45
Largest Number of Graduates
for "Graduation Bonanza!"
Thank You Villavicencio!

Day 5 – Page 57
Double Hitter Saturday!

Day 6 – Page 71
Double Hitter Sunday – Who Let the Cows Out?

Day 7 – Page 87
Team Goes Home-Time for a Big Roller Coaster Ride!

Day 8 – Page 103
The Gospel in the Wild West!

Day 9 – Page 117
Goodbye Big B. – Hello Mr. C

Day 10 – Page 129
Three Graduations and One Embarrassed Dean!

Day 11 – Page 145
The Andes Mountains
Make Colombia

Day 12 – Page 163
I am in Town Looking for an Anchor

Day 13 – Page 177
"Graduation Bonanza!" Comes to a Close
But it is Just the Beginning!

Day 1

Blessed Coming In and Going Out – It's a Blessing Day!

With a kiss and "I'll see you soon," I get into a taxi. Marjorie and I both hold back tears as emotions swell. We wave goodbye to each other as I disappear into the traffic filled streets of San Jose, Costa Rica.

Our children Rachel and Donnie have already gone to school. That makes leaving a little bit easier, but this will be a thirteen-day trip. It is much too long a time for me at this time in my life. It would have been more convenient to separate this trip into two parts to spend less time away from my family.

When I was a single man, I traveled two or three weeks at a time, and more than once I traveled four weeks at a time, but who would care? I only had myself to think about years ago. Wherever I was, it was home. I now have a wife and family; I can no longer be away from home for weeks at a time. There are too many family activities and commitments that I truly enjoy. I promised Marjorie when we married years ago, that I would not be away longer than fifteen consecutive days unless we traveled together. With only one exception, I have kept that promise. The exception was in 2001. I made a trip to Nigeria, Africa, and let me tell you, Africa was a long way from Costa Rica! Travel time excluding ministry was five days!

On this trip, I will talk with Marjorie one last time before leaving the country. Tradition says the phone at Gate Six is the *'last call home'* phone. Today I will make that call from my cell phone but not until I pass Gate Six.

Traffic appears normal for this time of day. I should be at the airport in about forty-five minutes. My flight is out of the (SJO) San Jose Airport but like a few other airports, (SJO) San Jose Airport is not located exactly where the name indicates.

In May 1958, (SJO) San Jose airport was relocated outside of the city. In fact, it was relocated outside of the province of San Jose. I always smile just a little when we land, and the pilot comes on to say, "Welcome to San Jose." The truth of the matter is that the airport is located in Alajuela, but for some reason, the name went unchanged. I sometimes wonder if it is confusing for the tourists. They land in San Jose and then travel by car another thirty minutes to an hour before officially arriving in San Jose. The good thing for me is that when I hear "Welcome to San Jose," I know I am almost home.

What is my destination for this thirteen-day trip? I am going to Bogotá, the capital of Colombia. This is not my first visit to Colombia or its capital. I have been there many times. Even so, I am always impressed by the country of Colombia and the fact that it is such a powerful place of ministry. The ministry has seen much fruitfulness and productivity in Colombia. For me personally, it is one of the most enjoyable places to visit. I love the nation and its people, and it is a joy to work with the local ministry team.

"Thanks for the ride," I say as I hand the taxi driver his fare. I situate my luggage and move inside. The line is not terribly long today, and it appears I'll be passing Gate Six in record time.

In just a few months, I will celebrate my thirtieth anniversary since moving to the mission field. As I stand in line looking at the airline counters, I remember the counter where I stood on January 9, 1984. That was the day I flew in to begin my life as a missionary on the foreign field.

My parents drove me to the airport. It is a three-hour drive from their home to (MSP) Minneapolis/Saint Paul airport. An early morning flight made for an even earlier drive, and it was chilly. The temperature was twenty-something degrees below zero Fahrenheit when we left, and the sun could not be expected to share its warmth for another four hours.

The car ride to the airport was especially quiet. This stands to reason since most people are not generally talkative at 3:30 a.m. However, this particular morning the undercurrent indicated silence would likely be the order of the day. It was common knowledge that both my parents enjoyed high hopes I would quickly outgrow my missionary aspirations and head for home. Their secret hope was that I would within a few weeks or maybe even months, be ready to find a "real job" and embark on a "real life" back in the states. So, to avoid saying the wrong thing before parting for such a length of time and distance, we rode to the airport in an uncomfortable silence sprinkled with a little, oh so little, small talk.

With boarding pass in hand and luggage checked, it was time to locate my gate. Though I would have a connecting flight through (MSY) New Orleans, I would not need to touch my luggage again until my arrival in (GUA) Guatemala. When I finished at the airline counter, it was time to leave the Lindbergh terminal and make my way to corridor C to locate the correct gate.

Mom has always been the tearful one in our family, and on this particular day, she did not disappoint. Emotions were high as I walked from the gate to get on the plane. Standing at the counter that day and then the subsequent walk to board the plane at the (MSP) Minneapolis/Saint Paul airport marked a change in my life that continues today.

When it was time to board the plane, there were only two things left to do; say goodbye and leave my winter jacket with my parents. I boarded my flight without a jacket, and they carried a little piece of me back home with them.

Eventually, my parents would come to accept the possibility I might be a missionary for the duration of my life.

Shortly after my departure, my parents ran into a business acquaintance. Within a few moments, my Guatemalan missionary status was brought into the conversation. When my parents most needed to hear encouraging words, their friend could only offer this; "Your son will probably come home in a wooden box." End of relationship....

"That truly was a dark day for us," my mother told me later. "We missed you terribly for months."

"We still do," Dad added. "We are very proud of you, Don, but during those first three or four months, we were increasingly lonesome for you."

A word from
Don and Sandy Korach Sr.

Thirty years now and oh, how things remain the same. It is still twenty degrees below zero in January in Minnesota, and I am still tearful when we say good-bye. Still, other things are quite different.

Don has a beautiful family, and his wife and children are wonderful. We love them so much! They are his family now – his support group. He is not alone, and that gives us, his parents, joyful hearts.

When he left that January 9th, I had only a phone number written on a piece of paper. It was the only way to reach him if he was needed. Yes, we wrote letters, but if we really needed him, we must call that number.

We didn't understand what he would be doing and knew nothing of his new home. Now we call Don, hear his voice and even visit with him and his family on Skype. It is wonderful – not as good as being together, of course, but it makes it so much easier to see and visit with each other.

We love Costa Rica. The country is beautiful, and there are flowers everywhere. It has beautiful mountains and awesome beaches. We have had many wonderful times in Costa Rica with Don's family.

Don has made Costa Rica his home. People know him everywhere he goes. He has touched so many lives. He cannot go anywhere without people greeting him. Both Don and the Bible Institute have affected so many people.

We are blessed. Costa Rica is truly Don's home now, and we are happy for him and his family. We miss them of course, but we are very proud!

Don and Sandy Korach Sr., Minnesota

"Yes, ma'am. Here are my ticket and luggage." A few moments later I am ready to stuff my boarding pass into my blazer pocket and pull my carry-on bag to the gate. *Thank God for luggage with wheels!* Now I only have two more lines to navigate before finding my gate; Passport Control and Security. Then, I will finally be on my way to Colombia.

In the spring of 1982, I was in one of these immigration lines for the very first time. A group of about forty of us went to Guatemala on a week-long trip during the Spring Break at Bible School. We were excited, and a little frightened as we deplaned and headed for Immigration. It didn't take long to notice things were different in Guatemala than in the United States.

Serious looking men standing shoulder to shoulder lined the hallway and rooms through which we passed on the way to Immigration. They were in uniform – and they all had rifles! We quickly noticed they weren't slouching or leaning against the wall. Nor were they chatting. They were standing at attention and alertly watching every move we made.

This visit was my first to a foreign country, and it would change my life forever. They kept our group quite busy. During the day, we worked to fence in a piece of property the ministry had recently purchased. We put up a barbed wire fence around the entire property in about three days and spent our nights attending a tent crusade the ministry was involved in at the time.

We helped with praying and other ministries of helps, but it was the missionaries who preached. As visitors, we watched carefully and prayed much. There were two tents; one for the adults and another for children. It was an enjoyable time of ministry for all of us!

I remember staying in a large house that doubled as an office for the ministry. While we were there, it served as a makeshift dormitory, and all of the men stayed in one long narrow room lined with six-inch thick pieces of foam along each side. My piece of foam was about a third of the way into the room on the right-hand side. There was one bathroom for everyone in the house and that one bathroom for all twenty-five men made for early mornings and long lines.

We completed the fencing project a couple of days early. It was originally scheduled to take all week, but we finished it ahead of time, and that provided us with the opportunity to do something unscheduled and quite rewarding. We visitors gathered an offering amongst ourselves to purchase materials to roof two little churches. We formed two groups and went to two separate locations; our goal was to roof both churches that day. One group of men went to the mountains. Another group went to the coast. I was part of the coastal team. We traveled down by bus and walked into the jungle with no more than some equipment and a little food for lunch. It was a long walk into a hot, muggy area.

Our team worked hard, but we had a great time. It was gratifying to complete that little country church roof in a day; actually two little country church roofs in one day! I viewed this as not only a workday but an adventure I'd always remember.

For the first time in my life, I saw banana trees. Don't ask me why but for some reason, I had always wondered how bananas grew. Well, I saw lots of them that day. I found out they grow upside down or at least in reverse of how I thought they grew. I also found out they do not grow on trees but on big stalks that feel similar to a corn stalk...a very large corn stalk.

The day before we were to fly out of the country back to the United States, a coup took place. Remember the soldiers in the airport? They were not there by accident. The coup was referred to as a 'bloodless coup', but that was not really true. Men did die, and due to that coup the airport closed. There would be no flight out the following day. Our departure was delayed, so we made good use of our time by holding a two-day prayer meeting; beginning the day of the coup and continuing through the day we were originally to leave Guatemala.

There was a lighter moment during that extra day that still makes me laugh. One of the missionaries had a few firecrackers and decided to ignite them during lunchtime. As you can imagine, it frightened some in the group. It sounded eerily like the 'ratta-tat-tat' we had heard the previous night during the coup! A few members of the group were quite alarmed, and the prankster found himself in trouble. His timing was terrible, yes, but the entire situation still makes me chuckle.

From this group of forty members about half became missionaries and served God on the foreign field, while the other half said, "Thanks, but no thanks." Still, their experience was a good thing. It is better to visit the mission field and discover what is truly in your heart, than to never visit and always wonder.

It was during this visit that God placed missions in my heart. It was never that God wrote across the sky and said, "Go to Guatemala or Costa Rica." Of course, a little writing in the sky would have been nice. However, with me, it has always been a knowing and confidence in my heart that said, "Welcome home...this is where you belong."

"Yes, sir. Here are my passport and ticket." The gentleman from Passport Control handed back my passport and boarding pass after checking that the name, photo, and face matched. I don't know what you think, but it seems this could prove a rather dull line of work. The day after day, monotonous checking of names in passports, on boarding passes, and verifying the face on the photo is the same as the person who just handed you all of those documents could become tedious. Though, I must say, on my last trip out I gained a new respect for those who check papers. The ladies at the check-in counter had mistakenly given me the wrong boarding pass. It was simple to correct now, but at boarding, it would have been much more complicated.

Back in the days of paper tickets, that happened to one visitor. For some reason, he was studying his airline tickets. I have never paid much attention to them. I would give the ticket to the person at the check-in counter, and they would pull out whatever they needed. On this occasion, as my visitor was looking through his tickets, he suddenly noticed he still had a ticket for a flight he'd already flown! Subsequently, he noticed he had no departure ticket for the upcoming flight! We called the airline and then realized they were already waiting for our call. They had found the ticket had been mistakenly pulled out in the last city. They were now flying it to us to make the swap. We had to make a trip to the airport to exchange tickets. It all seemed odd to me, but the airline acted as though it was a regular occurrence. In the end, no harm was done.

    Today all is well and in order as I walk around the etched glass wall to the Security Checkpoint. It is now time to take off my shoes, belt, and sports jacket. All of these items go through the x-ray machine along with my carry-on bag. As many times as I have done this, I wonder each time if I will be able to get through without a beep. *Have I forgotten a coin or pen or something? Have I missed anything that will cause beeping along the way?* This time, I made it through with no beeps, and I am cleared to go.

    Standing off to one side redressing, I realize I have finally gotten used to the security routine. Do I enjoy it? Of course not, no one does, but it has become a standard part of traveling. I find myself grateful for clear plastic bags and slip-on shoes that allow me to proceed toward the gate in record time.

    I see Gate Six and the payphone now. It is time to call Marjorie. We will touch base one last time regarding things at home. I assure her everything is fine at the airport. I tell her I arrived on time and that I am now past all security. If all goes well, I will be leaving in about an hour. Our last words to each other are simply: "*I love you.*"

    I relax a bit as I realize I have plenty of time to enjoy a cup of coffee before finding my gate. Fortunately, I can do so only two gates away. The Food Court is conveniently located at Gate Four. As expected, there are coffee samples available for tourists. This will be my last chance to purchase a cup of delicious Costa Rican Coffee. Of course, I do take advantage of a sample cup, along with a sample or two of chocolate covered cashews. I decide against indulging in chocolate covered coffee beans as I do not want to become too *wired* right before getting on the plane. Additionally, I find enough room in my carry-on to purchase a few items for my friends in Colombia.

Group B is called, and it is time to board the plane. I am out the door and up the steps, as they have us all go outside and walk across the tarmac to the plane. Not just this time, but every time, as I walk through the door of a plane, I touch the side of the plane and thank Father God for a safe trip. I remind the angels to prepare the way and that the camp is on the move. Today is a special day. It is a blessing day--a day of going out and coming in!

I find my seat is a letter D seat, which means it is an aisle seat. Aisle seats are my preference, and though it is a rare occurrence, I do not always get an aisle seat. When I do not, I know someone has made a mistake. I request the aisle seat because I like to move about without having to ask permission or step over others.

It only takes a few moments, and all are settled and ready to taxi out. The plane seems full with only a couple of empty seats on the opposite side. I always wonder where everyone is going but not today. Today, I know the answer. We are all going to Bogotá, Colombia. I chuckle to myself and thank God our destination is Colombia and not Nebraska.

No, I don't have anything against Nebraska. In fact, I have good friends in Nebraska, but a few years ago my family and I traveled to the States and experienced flight delays that etched Nebraska into our memory. Our original flight plan was easy; (SJO) San Jose, to (MIA) Miami, Florida, to (MSP) Minneapolis/Saint Paul. At least, it looked easy on paper. However, in living color, it wound up being much more

complicated. We left (SJO) San Jose late, which in turn caused us to miss our connection out of (MIA) Miami, to (MSP) Minneapolis/Saint Paul. We then had two options: wait until the next evening and fly out on the original flight-only twenty-four hours later or take an early flight out of (MIA) Miami to (DFW) Dallas and then on to (MSP)Minneapolis. We were anxious to see Grandma and Grandpa, so we decided the, sooner the better!

We left (MIA) Miami very early the next morning. The flight was on time to (DFW) Dallas; so far so good. We arrived in Dallas, made our connection, and it appeared we were only a few hours from Minnesota and the grandparents. A few minutes into the flight, one aisle in front of us, a man became ill. Very soon the man was lying on the floor right next to us.

We were situated in the last two rows of the plane. Donnie and I were sitting together, and Marjorie and Rachel were behind us. The flight attendants pulled out various medical instruments to attempt to help the gentleman. An announcement came over the loudspeaker requesting the assistance of any doctors on the flight. Immediately a doctor and a nurse made their way to the back of the plane to offer help. About the same time, the captain arrived. Bending down on one knee, he was able to get a better look at the sick passenger. He spoke briefly with the doctor and the head flight attendant and then hurried back to the cabin.

The captain immediately brought the airplane down from 30,000 feet and landed in about fifteen minutes! Fast and furious! On the descent, the airplane banked to the left, and I pointed out to Donnie what I thought was the airport. Sure enough, it was our destination, and we were quickly on the ground. By the time we landed, Marjorie had been moved to a row ahead of us, and Rachel was seated next to the window. The wife of the sick man was seated beside Rachel so that she could be close to her husband. This would make for a quicker exit after landing.

Emergency vehicles were immediately present when we landed. Police, fire, and paramedics, were lined up waiting with their lights flashing. They entered the airplane from the tail exit and within five minutes the sick passenger was on a gurney, out the door and zipping away in an ambulance.

I found myself impressed by all of the medical equipment kept on the airplane. I was also a bit surprised at how knowledgeable the flight attendants were concerning the use of the medical equipment. I was especially impressed at how quickly the paramedics retrieved the sick man from the airplane.

I thought to myself, "This isn't too bad. We will take off again in a couple of minutes, and this whole ordeal will amount to only about a thirty-minute delay." After all we had experienced the last twenty hours, a thirty-minute delay would be inconsequential.

Boy, was I wrong about that! It was an emergency landing in Nebraska and the problem with that was - we weren't supposed to be in Nebraska! It would be another two and a half hours before we took off again! Two of those hours we sat in our seats waiting for some official to come and check our airplane. The problem? We had landed in an overweight condition. The fuel that was supposed to have burned up between Nebraska and Minnesota was still in the wings when we landed. It would take an official inspection to make sure the airplane was safe enough for us to continue. Since we had made an emergency landing, they needed to make sure the airplane was not overly stressed or in need of repairs.

Approximately an hour into our waiting (inside the plane) our children - along with many other passengers – became a little fidgety. Rachel had a window seat so she could look out and see everything, but the excitement of this flight was *not outside the window. It had been on the floor right next to her! She had certainly had a close-up view of all the happenings, but all the commotion was now over, and she was sitting all by herself. As Rachel began to fuss, the flight attendant did all she could to keep her happy. How to do that? Food that was $5.00 a bag just a few minutes before was now at Rachel's disposal free of charge! It wasn't long before Rachel was handing food to the rest of us and sharing with others nearby in the tail end of the airplane.*

Eventually, we did leave (OMA) Omaha, Nebraska and arrived in (MSP), Minneapolis, Minnesota - two and a half hours late! Well, actually, it was twenty hours late according to our original plan!

That was then. This is now. As I lean back in my seat with a prayer and a smile, I say, "Thank You, Jesus, that this flight is headed for Colombia and not Nebraska."

Once through Immigration and Customs, I am out of the (BOG) Bogota, El Dorado airport and feeling the cool evening air.

Bogotá, the capital of Colombia, is a huge city stretching for miles in all directions. Some 10,000,000 call the city home, and with an altitude of 8,661 feet, the city is cool much of the time. In fact, Bogotá is the third highest major city in the world, following La Paz, Bolivia, and Quito, Ecuador. Because of the cool temperatures of Bogotá, the city has a pretty tight dress code. You will see all of the men walking around in dress suits and jackets, and I do mean all! It is not just a preacher thing. It's an everyone thing!

M.L., our ministry representative in Colombia and Pastor J.J., a pastor friend are waiting for me. It will take about an hour to reach Pastor J.J.'s home where I will stay while in Bogota. As Pastor J.J. navigates traffic, M.L. and I go over needed schedule changes and adjustments. We will have plenty of time to chat about the ministry later, but at the moment, my main concern is the smooth execution of events over the next forty-eight hours.

Pastor J.J. and I return to the airport later in the evening to pick up some of our visitors. We have two ladies and three gentlemen who will be sharing in ministry the next few days. The ladies' flight was on time, and we left the airport with no delays. The men will arrive tomorrow.

In only moments, they are all checked in at the hotel. I ask the ladies to rest up because tomorrow will be busy. We will go over the details, but right now we are all tired and need to get some rest. I leave them with a few simple instructions before leaving for Pastor J.J.'s home. "Ladies, remember; the conference starts at 9:30 in the morning. I will pick you up at 9:00 a.m. and take you to the conference location. Be sure to have breakfast before I see you. They serve a breakfast buffet from 6:30 to 10:00 a.m. in the restaurant on the first floor. See you in the morning!"

It has been a good day. Sometimes traveling days can be quite complicated, but we have had no problems. I was told years ago that you have to believe God to get in and believe God to get out. Well, on this day, we have been blessed getting in, and we will continue to believe we will be blessed going out!

Day 2

A Day for Ladies Only Ministry!

Today is our first full day in Colombia. Last night, our visitors from the States settled comfortably into their hotel, and I had a wonderful night's rest at my friend Pastor J.J.'s home. Staying at someone's home is something I have often done. It is usually quite enjoyable. True Colombian hospitality makes it exceptional!

As I sit down to breakfast, I breathe in the aroma of fresh Colombian bread, eggs frying, and of course, some of the best coffee ever brewing in the kitchen. Colombian coffee assures me it will be a great day! As I reach for some fresh papaya, a wave of memories washes over me as I recall some of the things that happened to me during my first couple of weeks in Guatemala.

Upon arrival in Guatemala, someone from the ministry team was waiting for me at the airport. We then traveled three hours to the ministry campus. The property we had fenced in on my first visit now had two buildings on it. One of the fellow missionaries had a birthday. That was when I learned that fireworks are a regular part of birthday celebrations in Guatemala. What a fantastic place where you can enjoy fireworks more than once a year!

That first weekend in Guatemala I traveled a couple of hours to meet up with the ministry team. One of the group planned to preach and show a movie. The drive to this church was beautiful and very mountainous. It was much different from where I was only hours before. In Minnesota, everything was white with snow. Now I was surrounded by everything green and tropical.

The church seemed to be located in the middle of nowhere but surprisingly it was packed full of people. There were so many people that there was a crowd standing around the outside of the building looking through the windows. I use the term windows loosely since the people on the outside were looking through holes in the building where windows should have been.

The movie to be shown was an evangelistic movie called, "Black Gold." It was a movie about T.L. Osborn preaching in Africa filmed in Nigeria many years ago. When it was time to show the movie, we realized the catch reel was back at the ministry base. What do you do now? Do you just say, "I'm sorry" to an overflow crowd? We must do something, but what? A quick decision was made to let the film fall carefully into a cardboard box, and the day was saved! We were well aware that a knot or tangle could mean the end of this powerful evangelism tool but decided it was important to forge ahead. After the service, we reeled it, oh, so carefully back onto the original reel and packed it away in its protective box. I learned quickly that improvisation is an integral part of the life of a missionary.

We had traveled quite a distance to the church. It was late by the time the service was over and the unrest in the nation made it unsafe to return, so we stayed overnight. The ladies slept at the pastor's home and the men in the church building.

Since I had just arrived, I was prepared with a sleeping bag. When I rolled it out to sleep on the floor, I was quickly advised to put a couple of benches together and sleep up off the floor. It was a better choice to sleep a few inches off the floor than to risk waking up with bugs and creepy things from the floor crawling all over you!

On my second weekend, the opportunity to help presented itself in an interesting way. After all, helping was the reason I was there. If and when I was asked to do something, I was ready to step in wherever I was needed.

A fellow missionary had double-booked himself and since it was impossible for him to be two places at one time I was happy to help him fulfill one of his ministry obligations. It sounded easy enough. All I had to do was take a film to the church service and bring it back afterward. Oh, and I had to make sure that catch reel was taken! Sure, I had learned a few days earlier that a cardboard box could do the job in a pinch, but the proper equipment makes an easy job even easier.

As I said, my assignment was simple. Take a film and projector to church for the Sunday evening service. My dilemma? How will I get there? I had been in Guatemala only a short time, and I scarcely knew where anything was located. Some relief came when I realized the pastor of the church would travel with me back to his church. Fair enough.

On Sunday afternoon, the local pastor who was to be my guide showed up right on time at the ministry office to travel with us to his church. The gentleman was an employee of the ministry as well as a local pastor. A fellow U.S. citizen who was visiting for a few days also traveled with us to the church.

The vehicle I was entrusted with was a brand new Mitsubishi van. The ministry had just purchased three new vans, and I was blessed to be one of the first drivers. The hour and a half trip to the church was rainy but uneventful. By the time we arrived at the church; the service had already begun. Like the last service I had attended, the church was packed full with people. However, due to the rain, no one was standing outside looking through the 'windows' this time.

As the pastor took the film and equipment into the church to set up, I had the bright idea to turn the van around. Turning around would make for a quicker departure after the service. It seemed a good idea at the time, so I went down the road a block or so away from the church to find a wide spot on the dirt road to turn around.

By this time, the heavy rain had turned the dirt road into a slippery, muddy mess and in an instant, the brand new van slipped off the road and into the ditch. How embarrassing! My very first drive in the country and my first adventure into the countryside and I get the vehicle stuck in the mud! Still, I did learn something that day. If you're going to get a vehicle stuck in Guatemala, be sure to do it in front of a church full of people. I hardly had time to realize what had happened when the van was surrounded by helping hands. Someone inside the church had seen what happened, and even before I was out of the van to evaluate the situation, the men of the church stopped the service, ran outside and pushed the van back onto the road.

I was extremely embarrassed and almost equally as impressed. They never missed a beat! In a moment, they were outside pushing the van out of the mud and then right back inside to continue with the service. It was as though pushing a vehicle out of the mud and back onto the road was a normal part of the church service!

The service was long and by the time it was over and we packed the film and equipment, it was quite late. Still, we had to make our way back to Quetzaltenango. Driving up was easy; I had a guide. Going back would not be so easy. The pastor who guided me to the church was now home, and that meant I was faced with the task of getting us safely back to the ministry office in Quetzaltenango unassisted. It was now only the two of us, the visitor from the United States and myself. Though he was good company, his presence did not contribute much to the return trip because he didn't know the roads any better than I did.

The first twenty-five minutes or so of the trip back to Quetzaltenango went well. The rain had stopped, so it wasn't difficult to see. It was just dark. At one point, we came to a "Y" in the road, and I wasn't sure which way to go, so I stopped to ponder my options. A few seconds after stopping, our van was quickly surrounded by thirty to forty young men all carrying big guns. We were in guerrilla country, and I quickly realized they were none too happy about our presence in the area. As calmly as possible, I told my visitor, "Just stay in the car – and pray!"

The leader of the group shouted out orders to his men. As he approached the driver's side of our vehicle, he began angrily interrogating me. The more he pressured, the more indignant I became. After all, he and his men were neither army nor police and had no authority. If they had been regular militia or local police, I would have happily cooperated with them as I have on numerous occasions. However, at that time, Guatemala was at war with communist guerrillas who were attempting to take over the government. These guerrillas had already taken control of certain areas of the country.

The leader shouted at me, "Get out of the car!" I refused. He told me to give him the vehicle papers. Again, I refused. He was becoming irritated. So was I, but I didn't let him know it! "Then give me your passport or immigration papers!" Again, I refused.

About this time, I demanded, "Let me see your I.D. that gives you the right to stop me and investigate me!" He refused. I insisted. The verbal tug-of-war went on for what seemed more than an hour, but it was probably only a few minutes. Still, we were getting nowhere fast. Can you imagine the scene? Here we were in the middle of nowhere on a dark, lonely road, very late at night, in a war zone being threatened by a bunch of guys with guns. Beside me, my friend was praying. Beside my friend, so was I!

Suddenly, a man who had been standing in the background, behind the apparent self-appointed leader, spoke up and asked, "Where are you headed?" I told him we were returning to Quetzaltenango. He looked at the road we were on and looked back at the van. He then spoke one sentence that broke the impasse. As he pointed, he said, "Quetzaltenango is that way."

"Thank you," I said to the man in charge and I started the engine. The men in front of the van stepped to the side, and we drove away. The Lord had protected us, and no harm was done. We went our way, but I must confess, I was especially glad to see the city lights of Quetzaltenango brighten the sky as we came around the mountain and looked down into the valley. What a beautiful sight!

Earlier that day I was concerned about the dirty roads causing the van to need a wash. Later on, I was completely *embarrassed, not only that the van was dirty, but now it was also full of mud! I was hopeful the dirt would be the worst of it and nothing was broken from sliding off the road into the ditch.*

As I contemplated earlier events on the long drive home, I was quite thankful neither we nor the brand new van was sporting any bullet holes. After all, a little mud is not such a big deal!

Pastor J.J. takes me to the hotel to meet up with our visitors. I am not only blessed to be staying at Pastor J.J.'s home, but I am also blessed to have him as the interpreter for the day. I could interpret and have many times, but Pastor J.J. is quite fluent, and he is Colombian. I speak Spanish but not *Colombian*.

We discover the ladies ready and waiting in the lobby. This is a good thing because we are running a bit late. As we settle into the car, I update them on today's itinerary.

"Ladies! Good morning to you! I have already talked to M.L. this morning, and she says the place is full. Now, as you can tell, we are just a little late, so we will walk in, I will introduce you and then it will be time to preach. Any questions? Remember; there will be a break for lunch from 12:00 to 1:00 p.m. and everyone plans to be with you until 5:30 p.m. We are only a few blocks from the service. Let me remind you that tonight there will be another service from 7:00 to 9:00 p.m. The pastors wanted an opportunity to hear you, so we added a previously unscheduled service for this evening. Any questions?"

I make introduction for the ladies and leave them in the care of our local director. I need to take advantage of the morning and make a few phone calls to some pastor friends. I am not looking forward to being the only male at a ladies only meeting, and thankfully I'm not! Pastor J. J. is interpreting, but as I sneak out the back, I realize *he* is now the only male at the meeting. He will be fine. It is his church we are using for the meeting. I chuckle under my breath as the door closes behind me.

I meet everyone back at the conference location by 4:00 p.m. We are supposed to finish at 5:30 p.m., but I have already learned by phone that the service will conclude a little early. Now we will have time to get ready for tonight.

The conference has concluded, and all went well. We retrieve the ladies from the conference, and we are off to the hotel. As we travel, I have a question for the visitors. I already know the answer to my question because I have already checked in with my Colombian crew, but I want to hear my visitor's point of view firsthand.

So I ask, "Well ladies, how did it go?"

"Don, it was wonderful! The ladies were attentive, and the interpreter did a great job. We are very impressed with Colombia. Do you know how many ladies were with us today and how many of them were in the ministry?"

"Yes, I do," I said, "There were two hundred in attendance and all of them in the ministry. Tonight some of their husbands and other ministry team members will be with us. Tonight we will leave at 7:00 p.m. for the service. You don't have to be there for all of the praise and worship. That will give you a little extra time at the hotel. Tonight, I cannot stay for the service because the men will arrive. In fact, they arrive on the same flight as you ladies did only twenty-four hours later."

The ladies go up to their rooms to prepare for the evening service. I find it better to wait for them in the lobby. There is simply too much traffic to go home. Only minutes into my wait in the lobby I am offered something to drink. I am quick to request a cup of coffee. Colombian coffee is really good stuff! Don't tell them in Costa Rica, but I think Colombian coffee is better; after all it is mountain grown.

The ladies arrive in the lobby right on time and seem surprised to find me waiting to take them to service. When we arrive, it is basically a repeat of the morning meeting. When we walk in, the praise and worship team sees us and quickly wraps things up, so we begin preaching. I introduce the ladies and once again, I leave. My departure was for different reasons this time, but if I keep this up, the ladies are going to start wondering!

I remember the day one of my visitors began to question whether I should even be in the ministry. He was concerned that I did not like church and thinking about it a bit longer, he thought perhaps he should pray a salvation prayer for me. He came to this conclusion because we never arrived at church on time during his entire visit. I would plan our schedule so that we would arrive just in time to walk in, and he could begin preaching. We never arrived on time and certainly never arrived early. Finally, as his visit was concluding, he mentioned his concern to me. He was very upset. Understanding his concern, I told him it was no problem to arrive at the service right on time, which we then did. We arrived at the service at its correct starting time. Eventually, people began filing into the building. The first to arrive was the lady with the mop who finished cleaning the floor. The music team followed and began to set up their equipment. They then tuned and tested all of the equipment. By now, the building was about a third of the way full, and the music team began to sing. As people were singing, others were filing into the building. Within a half hour, there

was a nice crowd. The music team sang for an hour, and of course, they sang in Spanish, which my guest could not understand. In addition, they sang off-key the entire time. It was almost a bit painful, as it was also quite loud!

Then there were announcements, the receiving of the offering, etc. By the time it was time for us to preach, over an hour had passed, and my guest was exhausted. All of this before he ever began to minister!

On the way home after service, my previously upset visitor leaned over and said, "Don, we can go to the service tomorrow on your time."

Pastor J.J. is interpreting, so another driver gets me to the airport right on time. First, I need to confirm that we are at the right terminal. International flights arrive at two places in Bogota. I have learned to pay close attention to flight details because it can be confusing and quite frustrating if you and your party are at different terminals. Though, I must confess; I have experienced both--attempting to pick people up at the wrong terminal and also people waiting for me at the wrong terminal. Now, we are at the correct terminal. However, the flight is a few minutes late.

As I wait at the airport, I am reminded that having visitors takes a bit of planning and preparation. If someone visits alone, it is much different than if there is a group of people. The more people visiting at one time, the more important the details become. Something as simple as bathroom space can be complicated when one person becomes forty people.

Often I am asked why we even have visitors, but truthfully, the why is the easiest question to answer regarding our visitors. For Marjorie and myself, hosting others is almost automatic. I grew up in central Minnesota at "Birch Acres Resort." If you do not take excellent care of the people who are on vacation at a lake resort, you will be out of business quickly. Marjorie, on the other hand, is simply a natural. I can only say; she is truly gifted in hospitality.

However, when someone asks me the "why do I have visitors" question I never mention Minnesota or how sweet my wife is. The answer is easy. The way I understood my call to the foreign field was first by visiting. It was in a visit that God deeply sowed the desire for missions in my heart. So, when a visitor or group of visitors is with us, I often wonder if they will be my neighbor some day and live in the foreign field full time.

By way of a visit to Costa Rica, some of our visitors are now missionaries. Some are here in Latin America. Others are as far away as Africa and China.

The monitor informs me that the rest of my visitors, the three men, arrived only thirty minutes late. It takes a while to go through Passport Control and Customs so, about an hour later they are walking outside the airport and taking their first breath of cool Bogotá air. When I see them walk out, I thank God. I haven't lost anyone today.

With the men checked-in at the hotel, the entire ministry team is now present. The men will be able to rest in the morning as the ladies will continue with the last day of the ladies' conference. I encourage them to take advantage of the time to rest because the week's schedule calls for early mornings. I will meet with them for a late lunch. I will introduce them to the rest of the group, and we will go over the details of the next few days at lunch. The men are quite interested in how ministry went today, so I shared the good report. I inform them our first graduation is tomorrow night and remind them to be ready with their graduation gowns.

Day 3

Everyone Is Here –
Let the Fun Begin!

What a great way to begin a day! The entire ministry team is in country. Thank God! No more trips to the airport! I am always glad when I am finished with airport pick-ups. There will be another trip to the airport in a few days, but that is the return trip. Once people are checked in on the return, I always sigh a sigh of relief because it signifies conclusion and success. After that check-in, the group is the airline's responsibility, and my part is complete.

Some time ago, a group of pastors visited us in Costa Rica. A group of pastors from various states coming in on various flights made picking everyone up a bit complicated, to

say the least. In all, there were twenty people in the group; not too big, not too small. The challenge was in that they arrived on four different flights. With that many flights, it is almost inevitable there will be delays. You know the typical airline issues: mechanical problems, a shortage of flight attendants, missed scheduling for the pilots. And of course, there is always the weather. The list goes on as to what might cause delays for an airline flight.

With so many people, so much going on and so many details, it is even possible to lose track of someone. In fact, I once did. One of the team members with a particular group was somehow lost in the shuffle. He was my last arrival. He began his trip in New York, but the east coast was experiencing weather delays. They changed his flight so many times that I had no idea where he was coming from or when he would arrive. Oh yes! I was at the airport to pick him up, but he never arrived, and no one could locate him.

At about 1:00 a.m., I received a phone call from Keith Hershey in California. It was quite embarrassing! Keith said, "Would you go over to such and such hotel? Pastor arrived, and no one picked him up, so he checked into a hotel the taxi driver suggested. Go and see if you can find him." By 2:00 a.m. he was with the rest of the group and was just glad to be there; especially since this was the first time he had ever used his passport. He never blamed us for losing track of him. In fact, the pastor was quite nice about the mix-up. For me, it was a bit embarrassing and certainly not the best way to begin a mission trip, but in the end, everything turned out just fine.

When I organize an event, group or ministry trip, I always ask myself and those I am working with a question. Those accustomed to working with me understand that I want the answer in detail. My question? *How many moving parts are there?* The fewer moving parts, the better, because there is less to go awry. A good example is the seemingly simple charge of having five others and myself here in Colombia. It took three domestic flights and three international flights to get us to Bogota. It also took three trips to the hotel. If there were fewer flights, there would be less moving parts. Less moving parts equals less opportunity for something to go wrong.

Years ago, growing up on a resort, I developed a habit of nicknaming guests. Each week a new group of people would come in, and the challenge of learning everyone's name and remembering who it belonged to was quite difficult for me. My mother was able to meet the weekly challenge. I, on the other hand, began referring to them by nicknames that usually had something to do with what cabin they were staying in, or by the type of fish they came to catch. Some habits are hard to break, so every visiting group that comes to minister receives a nickname. The nickname may be very complimentary or perhaps not so complimentary, but it will surely prove to be descriptive and always defines the overall group.

Many years ago, I enjoyed the visit of the "Two Week Eternal Group." The size of the group was only six people. That is the same count we have here in Colombia. It should be easy,

right? Well, the group consisted of six preachers; similar to my situation here in Colombia with five preachers. The interesting thing, however, is that the "Two Week Eternal Group" wanted to preach in six different places at the same time every day, at least once, if not twice a day. "No problem!" I said as I saw all the ministry that could be accomplished in a short time. But boy was I wrong about that! This meant I needed six places to preach or teach, six vehicles, six interpreters, all at the same time! There were so many 'moving parts' that each day was an adventure. Oh, and the fun did not stop there! We also went to another country. We took a three-day quick trip up to Nicaragua. What a great idea to help our new Bible Institute and to introduce the group to another culture! The benefits seemed ideal for everyone involved, but there would be an eight-hour road trip up and then back again; not to mention crossing the border, which is always an adventure.

In short, there were many, many moving parts. We have had several visitors since this distinctive group, and we do love our visitors. Though now, we only do one country at a time, and no group visits more than eight days at a time.

Even as our driver makes his way through traffic as fast as he can, I know we are going to be late. I just hope it is not late enough for anyone to notice. Even with our current lateness, I am impressed with how the traffic has improved in Bogotá. A few years ago the city council of Bogotá and the nation of Colombia embarked on a project for the city called, '*Transmilenio.*' The idea was easy, but making it a reality was a huge undertaking. The project *Transmilenio* took the buses out of the traffic and placed them in a separate lane for buses only. When I first heard of this project I thought, *this is crazy! It will never work!* Boy was I wrong! Transmilenio made the city livable again. Doing an errand like shopping for groceries before could easily require two hours of sitting in traffic. Now it can be done in twenty minutes. This concept of Transmilenio has been incorporated in many cities of Colombia, and other cities throughout South America. Millions of dollars were spent to remodel the city, but it was worth every dime. As we head toward the hotel where the team is staying, my thoughts drift back many years to my very first visitors.

I had been on the field for about a year when Dillious and Bonnie Bowman, a couple of my supporters from Tennessee, made plans to come down and see the ministry for themselves. All I had to do was simply pick them up at the airport. At that time, I worked in Cartago, a good hour from the airport without traffic, and at least two with traffic.

I arrived at the airport as scheduled, and I learned there was a delay for their flight. To be certain, I went into the terminal upstairs at the airline office. You could do this back in 1986. Today, you are not allowed inside the terminal if you are not traveling. The delay was confirmed. Subsequently, they kept pushing the delay thirty minutes at a time on the monitor until it was now two hours late. Finally, they announced the flight had not only been delayed but was now canceled. Once again, I went up and personally spoke to the airline office, and they told me that my visitors were not even on the plane. They looked up my visitor's flight information and told me that though they had left Tennessee, they had missed their connecting flight out of Florida.

Now, what was I to do? I turned around and went back home and placed a phone call to their home. Of course, they weren't there, but I was able to talk with their associate pastor. When I shared the situation with him, he told me not to worry. "They have had a very busy schedule, and they may have stopped off somewhere before they got to Costa Rica to rest." I went to bed exhausted thinking, how strange! Can people really do that; just stop in the middle of their connecting flights and tell the airline they will continue tomorrow?

The next morning I receive a call from the Bowman's. "Where are you?" I asked. Dillious tells me they are in Heredia, Costa Rica, staying with a pastor. "But, you can't be in Costa Rica," I said. "The airport computer told me that you weren't even on the plane!" Clearly they were in Costa Rica; no matter what the computer told us.

A few hours later I met up with them in San Jose, and the matter was cleared up. They had come in on the so-called 'canceled' flight later that evening at approximately the time I was speaking to the associate pastor in the states. They stayed in the airport until the lights were being turned off. It so happened that they made friends with a local pastor on that delayed flight who was kind enough to take them to his home. From there, they had called me.

Fortunately, Dillious and Bonnie weren't frightened away by that first experience and have been back to the field many times. In fact, they have even visited Colombia on various occasions and been instrumental in helping us walk through doors that opened to us, not only in Costa Rica but Nicaragua and even Colombia.

A word from
Dillious and Bonnie Bowman

When we think of Don Korach - one word comes to mind – Faithful-- because that is what Don has been to the call of God on his life. In some ways, it is difficult to believe that twenty-eight years have come and gone since our first visit with Don in Costa Rica.

We count it a blessing to have been invited to minister alongside Don on a few occasions. We are also blessed to call Don and Marjorie our friends.

We have always been blessed and amazed by the good care Don extended to us when we traveled to Costa Rica, Nicaragua, and Columbia. He took the same care whether it was only the two of us or we had a group of twenty or more in tow.

Our first visit was way back in 1986. We were Don's first guests from the United States, and we still joke with Don about how he "lost" us at the airport. He, of course, found us the next day.

As we remember back to those trips, we are so grateful to God for supplying all of the things we needed for the trips: money, supplies, shelter, etc. One example was God's provision of the funds to build a church in the mountains in Costa Rica. Another example was the Pastor's conference in Nicaragua.

We want to say thank you to Don, Majorie, Rachel and Donnie for their sacrifice in allowing us to share in a small part of their lives and ministry. We will never forget all the great ministry times and visits over the years.

Don's ministry has touched so many lives, not only in Costa Rica but at our home and within our church family. We have taken many people on mission's trips with Don, and their lives have been changed. Some are on the mission field right now at various locations in the world.

We are truly grateful for the people God has brought alongside Don in recent years to help in ministry. It has long been a prayer of ours that he would always have the help he needs.

From our hearts, Don, we want to say THANK YOU, for allowing us to take part in your life and ministry in Central and South America. We will always cherish the great memories. Keep writing! You probably have at least a couple dozen more books in you!

Thanks for asking us to share,
Dillious and Bonnie Bowman
Tennessee

As I step out of the car, I see the ladies in my group waiting for me in the lobby. What a blessing! They are ready to go. Once they are in the car, we talk through the activities of the morning. "Great to see you this morning! I am sure you remember, but let me refresh you on the schedule. Similar to yesterday, you will have all morning for ministry. Remember that by 1:00 p.m. you will need to dismiss for lunch. Our local ministry leader M.L. will introduce you today. I am going to stay here with you but kind of hide in the back. I want to get some photos of the event. When I said dismiss for lunch, it doesn't mean we will be serving food like yesterday. You will need to end the meeting by 1:00 p.m. so people can go home and eat lunch. They will not return for an afternoon session. When we finish, we will meet up with the rest of the team that arrived last night and have lunch together. Did you see any of the guys at breakfast? No problem. We will be together for lunch. Ok. Here we are! Enjoy!"

The teaching went great, and there seemed to be more in attendance today than yesterday. The ladies dismissed on time, and the men were ready to be picked up. Today, I am taking them to one of my favorite places to eat in Colombia. It is a Colombian chain called *'Crepes and Waffles.'* The irony of this place is that Colombians are very proud of speaking proper Spanish, but this restaurant chain has an English name. The restaurant location we are visiting today is conveniently close to the church where the meetings are being held and the hotel where the team is staying. It is called Unicentro Mall. Though occasionally some are, this location of Crepes and Waffles is not free standing. It is located inside a mall.

Entering a mall area in Colombia with a vehicle can be a little intimidating. I know what is about to happen. My visitors have been to many malls but not to one in Colombia. I watch as they all look around with eyes of disbelief. We pull up to the entrance of the mall, and we are greeted by a man with a mirror on a pole. He walks around the vehicle looking for bombs. While he is doing this, another gentleman asks us to pop open the trunk so his dog can take a sniff. Once we clear security, we get to park the car and go inside. However, some are now not so sure they want to be here! I try to remind them that we are not back home anymore. Life is different in other places of the world. My dry humor, reminding them it is better to have the bother of extra security than to have a car bomb exploding is not helpful.

We are at the northern entrance; so, Crepes and Waffles is only three doors down on the right. They have a great menu, fairly priced and wonderful service. The entire team enjoys a great lunch and expresses hope they might return. With the team all together, we go over the schedule of their visit and remind them how things do have a tendency to change. Just like last night, an additional service is added that was not on the original schedule. They assure us they understand. Even with the best planning, change happens.

I haven't interpreted yet, but I know my turn will be coming soon. My mind rushes to when I first moved to Costa Rica from Guatemala and began an excursion into the Spanish language and the Latin culture. It has been an interesting journey with some uphill climbs and some downhill slides, but always a fun ride!

When I first moved to Costa Rica from Guatemala, Marvin's church was one of the first churches I visited. He and his wife Yamileth were a young couple with a three-year-old son. A few months after that first visit, I knocked on his door. The visit was to ask if it was possible to move in with him and his family for a few months while studying at the Spanish Institute. This is not something I took lightly. You don't just knock on someone's door and say, "Can I live here?" I had heard they wanted to rent out a room so; it was an issue I took to prayer. I figured if I was going to learn the Spanish language I would do it head on. I knew that learning a language was not only about words and phonetics, but included experiencing the culture. What better place to learn a culture and a language than with a local family? A few days later I moved into the spare bedroom.

I could not make the decision of where I would live without considering the ministry and its requirements, and let me tell you, it took some selling to get this to happen! Not everyone in the mission was happy with the idea. In the end, I had permission to live with the Leandro family during the first thirty days I was enrolled at the Spanish Institute. The Spanish Institute was a twelve-month course, but I obtained permission to go only the first trimester. It was a total of only twelve weeks. Learning the language was tough, and at the end of twelve weeks, I was pleased it was time for the class to end.

Even though studying Spanish was difficult, I had an advantage; my Costa Rican family. Learning in school is different than learning at home. Basically, we are the ignorant students in school, and the teachers are the great and wise ones. On the other hand, at home with family, no matter how many times our children wrongly speak a word or use bad grammar, we still love them and watch proudly as they improve every day. My Costa Rican family took me under their wing and helped me in every way they could. They listened intently to my version of Spanish but were always there to assist and encourage me.

When I moved in with them, I was introduced to a 'widow-maker.' It is a small electric device attached to the shower that becomes the showerhead. As water goes through, it is heated and is supposed to give you a hot, or least warm shower. The idea of having electricity right there in the shower is a bit strange, but a shower with a widow-maker is better than freezing to death in the shower! I burned one up the first month I was with them.

One time, I was taking a warm shower, and the device began to throw sparks. Before I could get it shut off, it burned all the insulation off of the wiring. The entire house was awakened by all of the popping and the burnt wire smell.

My permission to study Spanish expired at twelve weeks, but I continued to study with my tutors for a long time. My permission to live with the Leandro family also expired at thirty days. However, ministry and life were both quite busy, and it seemed no one noticed where I was living, so I never mentioned it again. I lived with Marvin and Yamileth and their three children for six years. They actually moved out before I did; moving to Nicaragua for a couple of years as missionaries. Later, while in Nicaragua, I visited Pastors Marvin and Yamileth several times. On one occasion, I was with them a month.

About two years after moving in with Marvin and his family, there was an international meeting of the entire missionary team. People came from all over Central America. I went to Guatemala for the week long meeting. One of the meetings included a report from each nation. I came prepared to tell about the changes we had made in the Bible School in Costa Rica and how successful it was, but that is not what others wanted to hear. Their interest and questions were not regarding the ministry but my living arrangements. "How was it," they asked, "to live in the home of a Costa Rican family?" A better question might be, "How was it for a Costa Rican family living with me!"

A word from
Pastor Marvin and Yamileth Leandro
The Visitor Who Came to Stay

Being pastors of a small congregation, we had the heartwarming visit of a young missionary from the United States, who worked with a foreign ministry. That young man's name is Donald Korach. When he visited us, he could not speak a word of Spanish. He had decided to live with a Costa Rican family to learn the language and culture. This decision was a great step for Donald. It allowed him to learn how Costa Ricans think and see the world. He learned our phrases and traditions regarding church, commerce, politics, and meetings.

Our family had the privilege of being chosen by young Donald. He was supposed to live with for one month. However, the month was happily extended to six months. During this period, we formed a great bond. He was adopted as one more member of our family. My children still think of Don as their "gringo uncle" who played with them as children. His friendship, esteem, and blessing will always be present in our family.

Marvin and Yamileth Leandro
Sr. Pastor Nazarene Bible Church
Costa Rica

These two weeks of ministry in Colombia have been officially named. No nicknames for this ministry trip; only groups and visitors get a nickname. We are calling this trip to Colombia *"Graduation Bonanza!"* Our first graduation of thirteen is this evening on the north side of Bogota. In fact, the graduation and the conference with the ladies will be held in the same place. When we arrive, we are met with students standing in one line outside the building being fitted with their graduation robes. From there, they go inside to another line to sign the proper papers of protocol. It looks a bit confusing to the untrained eye, but to me, it looks beautiful! All of these people have been touched by the Gospel because of the Bible Institute.

In a little while, anyone will recognize the event as a graduation, but as people ready themselves for the event, things look slightly out of order. As the graduates stand with their friends taking pictures, a few invite me step in the photos with them, and others ask me to take their picture. Some of the students have come as much as three hours early so that we may start on time. These Students have worked hard and have come to a place of transition in their lives from being students to graduates.

I direct the group to their seats in a reserved location in the front row. They want a good view of all the happenings. Many guests of the graduates are seated. I truly enjoy a graduation when the students can share it with their families. Some of the team members and myself head off to the pastor's office to change into our graduation attire.

As praise and worship begins, I am particularly pleased to see Pastor David and his wife leading the service. I met them on my last visit to Colombia. Both will graduate tonight.

I may be biased, but I believe our best music groups are always those who have participated in the Bible Institute. Additionally, the most handsome and beautifully dressed are those in graduation robes!

Anyone on the team can give a wonderful charge to the graduates, but tonight I am honored to introduce Pastor Dr. Dick Braswell, from Mobile, Alabama as the keynote speaker for the event. Pastor Braswell asked me how much time he had to preach. Wow! I never expected that! My response? Twenty minutes. In all reality, many pastors would never have asked. Though some may have asked out of courtesy and then still taken all the time they had originally wanted. Pastor Braswell not only asked, but finished his very powerful, anointed charge within those twenty minutes! I was very impressed, thinking, *What a great group I have with me!*

Tonight we have gathered eighty-four graduates from seven separate churches. What a wonderful way and beautiful place to begin *"Graduation Bonanza!"*

A word from Pastor Dick Braswell

I was privileged to be invited as one of the graduation speakers and teachers during the 2008 graduation exercises for the wonderful Bible Students in and around Bogota, Colombia. It was awesome!

The warmth and love we experienced coming from those who were involved in this life-changing ministry was indescribable.

The organization for this momentous task was outstanding, and the leadership demonstrated the anointing of the Holy Spirit in every aspect of this mission outreach.

The students were so enthusiastic! They were totally committed to following the Call they received from God in many and various ministry areas.

As I preached and taught, the messages were received with appreciation and gratitude. It was so refreshing to witness the families of those graduating join in celebrating and rejoicing with their loved ones...What a blessing!

I am encouraged by the assurance that those students to whom we handed out diplomas will carry the Word of God in power, not only to their nation but the uttermost parts of the world.

My hearty commendations to Dr. Donald Korach for a job well done and for the anointing he carries for this world-changing work. We will faithfully pray and believe God that this powerful ministry will continue to bless the nations of the earth.

Thanks again for allowing me to play a small part in touching the lives of so many brothers and sisters with the unchangeable Word of God in South America.

Pastor Dr. Dick Braswell
Sr. Pastor Life Church, Mobile, Alabama

Day 4

Largest Number of Graduates For "Graduation Bonanza!" Thank You Villavicencio!

Today is an exciting day! It is a travel day and begins as a very early day for all. The team members are loaded up in the van and ready to travel by 6:30 a.m. They have been busy this morning. They had to have their luggage separated into what would stay and an overnight bag to keep with them. Additionally, they had to be checked out of their rooms. I have a punctual crew, and we are all loaded up and ready to go right on time.

We are going to the city of Villavicencio, and the drive is unparalleled. We will be going out the southeast side of Bogota. There is very little traffic because of the early morning, but it will still take over an hour to cross the city. It will then take another couple of hours getting through the mountains.

Now, when I say through the mountains, I mean through them. There are seven tunnels to pass through; some short and others over three miles long. A very impressive engineering feat, this road, is known as the new road. The old road that goes over the mountains is a twelve-hour drive but is a very picturesque and enjoyable journey.

Villavicencio is the capital city of the Department of Meta. In the United States, we have states. In places like Canada or Costa Rica, they have Provinces, but in Colombia, they are known as Departments.

The climate of Villavicencio is easy to describe; HOT. We will go from the cool, high altitude city of Bogotá to the low-lying, tropical climate of Villavicencio in just three hours. When you come out of the last and one of the longest tunnels, you see the beautiful plain that stretches around the Andes into Venezuela. For me, this is always a wow moment! Villavicencio is situated to the east of the Andes Mountains and is called the 'Gate to the plains.' This is the plain that lies between the Andes range and the Amazon rainforest. Because it is located in the foothills of the Andes, the morning and evening breezes cool the city and give it some relief from the hot day.

Relief has a great sound to it. Not everyone is easy to work with, and I would have welcomed a bit of relief as I was baptized by fire during our first big project of the ministry.

After living in Guatemala for six months, I moved to Costa Rica. One of the first things I did was help organize a Bible School. The Ministry knew they wanted to teach and train people, but had no well-defined idea what to do. The question

before us was: should the Ministry only teach in churches, or should we develop a Bible School curriculum with a specific goal in mind? Finally, another couple and I were given the assignment to prepare a curriculum. So we began working.

We met at their house on Friday and worked throughout the weekend. Our immediate task was to decide what courses to teach and why; how long the courses would be, and who would be our potential students.

By Monday morning, we had completed a 'Bible Institute Proposal.' We had no idea if it would be accepted, adjusted, or simply rejected. I fully expected it to be adjusted because it seems almost everyone likes to put his or her personal touch on a project. They usually do this by making simple revisions, but may do so by changing the original proposal so much it is almost unrecognizable.

Our first proposal was rejected outright. The missionary couple that had worked with me over the weekend had fallen in love with the proposal and sensed its potential effectiveness. However, when they presented the plan to the Ministries Director, they unwisely told him, "Take it as it is, or we are leaving." It took the director only about thirty seconds to make a decision, which was, "Pack your bags. We will not do it as is; so, you can leave."

What a blow! I was disappointed in the way they had presented the proposal, and even more disappointed in how the director reacted. A few weeks later, the couple had left the field, and I was left wondering what I would do. In the end, the director again asked me to present him with a Bible Institute proposal, which I willingly did, simply by changing the cover page of the original proposal. The director approved the 'second' proposal with no changes or adjustments at all.

Since then, the paper tiger we sweated over that weekend has proven to be a very effective part of the Ministry and a powerful tool in the making of disciples for the Kingdom of God. How disappointing that the other couple was never allowed to be a part of the success of it. Their immaturity and the director's lack of leadership in the matter destroyed their lives as missionaries in under a. minute. Lord have mercy on our souls!

We have a tight schedule, but we have enough time to stop for a quick breakfast. We stop at a place that is no more than a gas station with a little restaurant. It was a simple place, but it seems clean and has a great view of the mountains. Once we arrive at the hotel, we have to get moved in and go over to where we will teach. We are due to begin teaching at 10:00 a.m. There is no time for lollygagging.

Once again, everyone does a fantastic job getting checked in and ready. We promptly arrive at the church where we will have the Pastor's Teachers Conference until 5:00 p.m. We will then hold the graduation at 7:00 p.m.

Today, I stand aside and let my visiting team members teach all they want. They have come to minister, so I encourage them to go for it. I will have all next week teaching alone, so I appreciate the help today. I also appreciate that we have come a long way from our first classes back in Turrialba, Costa Rica. What a crazy and memorable day that was for everyone involved!

I had been on the foreign field for less than a year when I had an opportunity to teach in our Bible Training Center. The location for this training center was to be the first one where we

operated as an extension school. Up to this point, all students had to come to us at our home base. I was convinced that an extension school would create a larger student body. Like most things, it took a while for the rest of the ministry team to embrace the vision.

The extension school pilot project opened in the city of Turrialba. Turrialba is about a two-hour drive from our home base city of Cartago. It was one of the first cities away from Cartago that the Lord opened for the ministry. It was the first city in which the tent was used for evangelistic crusades. So, it was a natural progression to do the pilot project extension program of the Bible Teaching Center in that city.

Turrialba is a key city on the eastern side of the country. It originated because of the train. It became the last big city in which the train stopped before climbing the mountains into the central valley and on to Cartago and San Jose. Along with the influence from the rail, it is also a college town with students coming in from other Central and South American nations.

Once the pilot project began, it wasn't long before I was able to schedule myself into the teaching roster. I remember getting up early on Saturday and driving the foggy, windy road to Turrialba. The drive has an amazing scenic view, with small towns scattered among the coffee fields. Less than half an hour away, the climate and fields change from coffee to sugar cane. Just as I descend into the City of Turrialba and onto the plain that takes you all the way to the Caribbean coast, I stop at my favorite truck stop for a quick breakfast. Classes begin by 8:00 a.m., so I have about forty-five minutes for breakfast and one last look at my notes.

Upon arriving at the pilot project location, I see all of the students are present and ready to go. The theme for the day is faith. We will have five hours of teaching with an hour for lunch and fellowship. If all goes well, we will be heading back home around 2:00 p.m. This will allow the students to return home before it gets too late. Today I am not the interpreter, but I have brought someone to interpret for me. These are the early days of my time in Latin America, and fluent Spanish is still out of my reach.

As we begin teaching, all is going well. The students are asking good questions, and nothing seems to be out of the ordinary. On the Second hour of our teaching, the interpreter is standing to my right, and I am about half way into my hour of teaching. Then I see something I have never seen before. I look not at the students in front of me but past them to the back of the building. Standing in the door of the church is a young man with his shirt off. Shirt or no shirt is no big deal. Turrialba is a very hot place. However, he is holding a buck knife in his right hand, and he is cutting across his chest. As you can imagine, someone slicing up their chest with a knife will garner attention. My interpreter and I both stop mid-sentence and move toward the young man. We, along with the students, lay hands on him and pray as we cast the devil out of him. In only a few minutes, he is set free. As he came back to himself, he had no idea where he was, how he got to the church, or that he had been mutilating himself.

What a powerful way to begin a pilot program. The news of this young man being set free went throughout Turrialba. The church that was letting us use their building instantly grew, and the following month we had new students wanting to study with us!

As I get out of the van in front of the church, I immediately recognize the location. It looks much different than the first time I saw it, but I know exactly where I am standing. The first time I came to Villavicencio was for our first graduation in the city. We held the graduation in one of the meeting rooms at the hotel where we are staying tonight. On that first trip, after graduation, one of the pastors took us to an empty lot they were about to purchase for his church. He asked us to pray over the property, which we were happy to do. Now, we are standing in front of a beautiful church building that holds roughly five hundred people.

The facility is amazing, and the ministers give the students and ear full of great teaching. Some of those attending live close enough to their homes to go home and get ready for the graduation. Others simply hang around and fellowship after the conference while they wait for the graduation to begin. I have a great time talking with and sharing some quality time with a few of my pastor friends in the area.

Since my first visit, I have returned for conferences and graduations in this city and the surrounding area. I have had the opportunity to preach in some of their churches. For me, visiting Villavicencio is like hanging out with my buddies. One of my pastor friends tells me his church is holding a crusade in a tent, which is always exciting! It reminds me of my experience with our first tent years ago.

What an exciting weekend! The ministry received money to purchase a tent. After some investigation, it was decided not to have a tent shipped in but to have a tent maker bring in the pieces and put it together in country. I later learned if we had brought it in assembled and ready to go the import taxes would have been exuberant and the permits to nationalize it would have

taken forever and a day. The tent maker arrived with the pieces and his equipment to weld, not sew the pieces together. His luggage did get caught and sent to customs to pay a tax. The following day, the tax bill was paid for the material, and it was time to make a tent. He knew what he was doing, and by the end of the second day, all the pieces were ready. Now it was time to find poles, stakes and lots of rope. You don't just go to the hardware store to purchase tent pieces. We did find the rope we needed, but we had to shop two different hardware stores. The side poles were prepared for us at the lumberyard. The two center poles were specially made in a welding shop. Where did we find the right material for all of those stakes? To my surprise; in a junkyard! It took a few days, but in less than a week, the tent was up and looking nice. That tent was used countless times over the next few years and throughout Costa Rica to preach the Gospel and help bring in a harvest of souls.

Then, there was my first crusade. The very first time we used the tent was in Turrialba, but I didn't have much to do with that crusade because I was still at the Language Institute. The first time I set up a crusade with the tent was in Ciudad Quesada. Ciudad Quesada is in the province of Alajuela and is the main city in North-Central Costa Rica.

I knew what we needed for the crusade. First, we must have access to a lot both large and level enough for the gathering. It must be a place people can find and of course, a place where the tent would fit. Second, we needed permits from the local municipality. Last, but not least, electricity; mostly for the lights and sound equipment. We already had some churches interested in taking part in the crusade.

In our early meetings, I was told a crusade like we wanted to host was difficult to set up and would take various *trips and probably months to prepare for; if we could do it at all. That is partly why the job fell to me to spy out the land and see what we might do. I was told outright by others that it was too much work, and they were fearful of the whole idea of doing a crusade there.*

After some prayer and preparation time, it was time to go to Ciudad Quesada and see what could be done. I arrived there a day early in late afternoon. I found a lot that would work perfectly for the tent, and a neighbor was happy to supply all the electricity we needed. I obtained a verbal commitment from the municipal office that permits would be given in a few days. Boy, did I enjoy going back to the office with this report! Our fearful friends were encouraged by what the Lord had done, and instantly they became great men of faith! The crusade itself went on for several weeks and produced much good fruit.

It was through the crusade in Ciudad Quesada that I was introduced to and worked with a young pastor in the city named Abdenago Piedra. We all call him Nago. Thank God because I don't think I could even say Abdenago the first time we met! Nago is a dear friend. Even though we come from totally different cultures and settings, the Lord has put our lives together in an exciting way. When I came to the field, I was single. He was also single. He married his wife six months before Marjorie and I were married. He has two girls and a boy, and I have one of each. We still see each other often because of the ministry. He often helps teach some of our classes in the Bible School.

A word from V.R.E.

Another man that was a major help in all of this was Brother Gamboa. He had a jeep, and he did a great deal for us. God had healed him, and he was so grateful that he was up and down San Carlos helping however he could. Like most things on the mission field, teamwork is required. I was a first-year female missionary who spoke some Spanish, and I was ready to help hands-on or however else I could help. We also had a group from Cartago, from Pastor Vega's church that made the trip to San Carlos to help set things up and keep them running smoothly. Anyway, I was asked to pray for a lady with a tumor who lived in the house where they let us hook-up to their electricity. The woman was in bed when we arrived. I invited a couple of young brothers from the church in Cartago along to pray. I prayed with conviction knowing Jesus is the Healer! I found out several days later that the Lord had healed the lady, praise God!

We invited a Brother who helped with the teaching ministry in the various locations to be the interpreter for the crusade. He was from Panama and was a Professor at a University.

Working in this ministry was challenging for various reasons. Good leadership and unity are key in any ministry, but when leadership does not consider the team and/or walk in the Fruit of the Spirit, the challenges increase a hundred-fold. The director would often have fits of rage and yell at those who were there to serve the Lord whole-heartedly. I was advised shortly after joining the team that if I ever saw a fellow-missionary brother flying through the second story window, that I was to mind my own business. Fortunately, the other missionaries, Mr.

Korach and I worked well together and supported each other in order to accomplish the vision of the ministry. God is good and despite the trying times, we kept our hearts pure and our eyes focused on Jesus. He is the Author and Finisher of our faith, and HE alone was our reason for being on the foreign field.

V.R.E.
Co-Worker in Costa Rica
During the 80's and 90's

The graduation tonight is similar to last night; complete with graduates and guests arriving - only more of them. They will go through the same *obstacle course* as last night in order to sign all of the proper documents and retrieve the right graduation robe. Tonight, we will have our largest graduation of *"Graduation Bonanza!"* One hundred forty-six graduates have gathered in this new facility. They are from ten different churches in the area. By the time the praise and worship team sings the first note, the building is packed with graduates and their guests.

Tonight, I not only get to introduce the commencement speaker but take a few minutes to talk with the graduates. There are a few things I like to do in every graduation, and tonight is no exception. I want everyone to relax and be encouraged, so this is what I tell them.

"As your Dean, this will be the last time I speak to you as students. As you may or may not know, there will be one last exam before we hand out the diplomas." There is always a gasp as they all look at me and each other wondering why no one had told them about the exam. I assure them that if we were in Costa Rica, someone would already be handing out papers and pencils. I say, "However, M. L., the Colombian representative of the ministry, has stepped in and interceded for you so that no test will be given." The graduates roar and applaud for their now much-appreciated director!

Then I ask all the students to stand up, turn around, and face their wives, husbands, children, parents, and friends. I remind them that this day we are here celebrating their graduation, but they did not get here alone. They arrived here with the help and support of their family and friends. The graduates are always quick to show thanks by applauding for their families and friends.

I do have the honor of presenting Dr. Roger Price. He is tonight's commencement speaker. Dr. Price has been with us since the very beginning. He was the commencement speaker at the charter graduation in Costa Rica. He was also was with us on the first trip to this city when we prayed for this building when it was but an empty lot. As I hand him the microphone, he reminds me that the platform we are standing on that overlooks the graduates is the very spot we were standing when he prayed years earlier.

It truly has been another great day! There was teaching time with students and a wonderful graduation service. Graduations are always fun, but when they are this big, they are exceptional! As I'm sure you realize, it takes a while to hand out this many diplomas and to take pictures. The entire crew gets involved and helps. We all finally finish and go back to the hotel to rest up. Tomorrow will be a double header!

Day 5

Double Hitter Saturday!

Today is Saturday, and it will be another busy day as we have a double hitter scheduled in Bogota. We have a couple of graduation services scheduled; the first one at 2:00 p.m. and another at 7:00 p.m. I can only anticipate great things as we continue our *"Graduation Bonanza!"*

We wake up in Villavicencio knowing that after breakfast we will be traveling back up the mountain we came down yesterday.

I am blessed to meet with a couple of pastors before leaving for Bogota. The team is up and moving. They check themselves out of their rooms and load the van as I sneak over to the restaurant for breakfast.

As I get into the van and lean back in my seat, I realize just how much I dislike the van we are traveling in. It has worked fine for getting to various locations but is not very comfortable. I know it will bounce and throw us around as we work our way back up the mountain. Then there is our driver, who loves to swerve around corners and keep us praying as we all wonder if we will make it safely back into our lane each time he tries to pass another vehicle.

As we go through the mountains, we see what looks like a terrible accident. The car is all twisted up. It looks as though some people are still in the car, and some were thrown from the car. It is quite and impactful sight. As we get closer, we can better see what has happened. The police have placed a badly wrecked car on the side of the road and placed manikins in and around it. The sight of this would slow anyone down. Well, not everyone; not our driver. He is driving back home and wants to set a record! Have you ever ridden a horse that knows where the barn is? Our driving experience today is like we are on our way to the barn-full speed ahead!

We arrive at the southern entrance of Bogota in what seems like record time. My team is quiet on the return trip. Between the heat, the traveling time and ministering everyone is a bit tired. It makes for a quiet ride back. Remember how your parents always said if you would sleep the trip would go faster? Well, it sure worked for us that day.

We find we have no extra time on our hands. The group must unload the van and get settled into the hotel since there will be no more moving around for the remainder of their visit.

About a half hour before arriving at the hotel, we dropped off M.L., so that she could get home and arrive on time for the graduations. We will meet up with her later at the first graduation service.

We have a lot to do before leaving for our first graduation of the day. To accommodate today's schedule of events, we will have a late lunch or an early dinner between the two services. I have already checked, and there is a Crepes and Waffles restaurant near the location of our last service. As I mentioned before, it has delicious food, and everyone is willing to wait.

As the team gets settled at the hotel, I go back to Pastors J.J.'s home to get ready. The only one who doesn't have time to go home is the driver. He waits while Pastor J.J. and I get ready. He will then take us back to pick up the team, and we will head to the first graduation. He will have a chance to sneak away while we are at the graduation ceremony.

When I arrive at Pastor J.J.'s home, my phone rings. Someone back home is calling. "Hello, Rachel. How are you doing?" I talk with Rachel and Donnie as well. It is good to hear their voices and learn that all is well back home. As I hang up, I laugh because it reminds me of what they said about me when I was in Panama recently.

I call home from Panama to tell Marjorie I am going to be live on television in about seven minutes. I tell her, "If you go to the television's web page you can see the live feed."

"Ok," she says, "the kids will get it up and working."

We are the pastor's guest in this live telecast. The pastor walks into the studio as they are counting down. "Ten, nine..."--It is only then the pastor tells us we are going to talk about faith tonight---"Three, two, and one! Welcome to the program!" And for the next hour and a half we talked about faith. The Pastor asked us questions, and people called in with questions. It proved to be an impressive program.

The next morning I talked with Marjorie, and she told me that they could only hear the program, but not see it. It was some technical problem. As they listened to the show, they, of course, recognized my voice. As they were listening, Rachel said to her mom, "That can't be Daddy, because whenever we ask him a question here at home he always says the same thing. Ask your mother!"

A word from Rachel Korach

Being a missionary's kid isn't that different from being a regular kid. I do not feel like I live in a foreign country because I was born in Costa Rica. However, I do get to meet people from all over America. The constant visitors are usually fun to hang out with, and I learn more about God with their testimonies and prayers.

Dad is not only a missionary but also a teacher in the Bible Institute. His involvement has inspired me to become a teacher in the future. I want to build a Christian school in Guanacaste, and bless the people in that region with a good and affordable education.

God has healed me and taken care of me since I was born. He has blessed mine and Donnie's life with great parents that always have time for us. They have helped us every step of the way, and I am very thankful for that. I know it is not easy for a missionary and a homemaker to take care of two kids, but they have done an amazing job! They have made sure we received the best education to succeed in the future. I'm going to miss them a lot when I go off to college.

Rachel Korach

A word from Donnie Korach

Growing up with a missionary dad is pretty interesting. We usually get two or three groups that come in every year. Those groups coming in is my favorite part of the ministry because we get to meet new people, and they are all different. Some are very nice; some are serious, and some are funny and fun to be around.

My favorite story of having a group with us was the time that dad was doing a conference. He had to go to Nicaragua and get the conference ready over there, but the group that was in Costa Rica stayed one day without him. Rachel, Mom, and I took care of them. We took them to Volcano Irazu. It was a great day to go to the Volcano because it was not cloudy, and we could see it. The volcano was beautiful; everybody liked it, and then we had lunch at the mall.

We headed back to the hotel by 4:00 p.m. so everybody could rest up and take a nap. After a couple of hours, mom called KFC for dinner. I went and knocked on their doors and told them that we had chicken. When I got to one of the rooms, one of the ladies was missing. I told mom, and she said that she must be walking around the building. So, I went outside and looked for her. She wasn't around, so I told mom that she wasn't there. We all got a little nervous. It was 8:00 p.m. and she was still missing. Suddenly we saw her arrive in a police car and walk in like nothing had happened. The leader of the group asked where she went and why she had left like that. All she said was that she saw a chicken restaurant she had seen on the way to the hotel and that she wanted to check it out. On her way there she got lost, so she asked a police officer to take her back home. Here is where it gets interesting. How did she tell the police officer where she was staying if she did not speak Spanish, and he did not know English? She never told us. The worst part is that we had ordered chicken!

So, being the son of a missionary isn't boring. It is fun! However, the guy that makes it fun is dad. Dad always keeps the groups busy, and he is great at it. I love him a lot. Mom is also very helpful. She is the best cook in the world, and I do not know what I would do without her. I wouldn't change my life as the son of a missionary. I like it a lot!

Donnie Korach

We arrive at the first graduation a bit late and one team member short. One of the men said he needed a night to rest up. I think it is good that he has enough sense to rest up a little. Years ago, I would have had a fit and told him that he would have to go. We are a team you know. That is nonsense. I let him rest. Tomorrow is another day.

When we arrive, I can tell right away, even before entering the church that there is a problem. Something is amiss. There is no music playing. As I walk in, I see everyone dressed in their graduation robes, seated and waiting to begin. I discover we were not the only ones to experience a traffic delay; so did the music person. M.L. has obtained all the proper signatures in the proper places, so we decide to start the graduation service without the music person. Once again, I open with prayer and greet the students. Of course, I am tense about having everyone wait, but they were patient, and since the graduation exam was canceled, they are forgiving. This graduation has ninety-nine graduates from eight different churches. Our ministers deliver a wonderful charge to the graduates.

When it is time to hand out the diplomas the person leading music finally arrives. Instead of doing music prior to the graduation, we do it near the end. Perhaps this is not the best way to do things, but we are missionaries, and we have learned to improvise.

At all graduations, we like to give the graduation caps a toss into the air and of course, the graduates love it. At this church, there is a balcony, so the ceiling is extra high; perfect for the toss. "Ok everyone! Ready?! One, two, three! Hallelujah!"

On another trip to Bogota, the graduation cap toss almost tore the building down!

We pulled in and found a reserved parking place. The occasion was a graduation in Bogota. I went up the stairs to the second floor and the main sanctuary. The place was already full of people with just over a hundred graduates and as many friends and family members. The music was excellent! I gave a charge to the graduates. Once we finished handing out all of the diplomas, it was time to throw graduation caps.

"Ok. I am going to count to three and on three, we will throw the caps with a shout of Hallelujah! One, two, three, Hallelujah!" But when the caps came down, they did not come down alone. Some of the caps hit the hanging ceiling in such a way that tiles came crashing down on top of the graduates. It was hilarious! Well, I thought it was hilarious, but the local pastor was not so happy! I assured him we would pay for

damages. Interestingly, now that I think about it, we haven't used that church again for any graduations.

As the music starts, the now-graduated students celebrate, and we leave in a hurry as we need to get to our next graduation. M.L. goes directly to the graduation location to do all the preliminaries, and I have the burdensome chore (ha-ha) of taking the team to lunch that now looks a lot like supper. Fortunately, Crepes and Waffles has both English and Spanish menus. My days of translating menus and ordering food for people has long passed!

During one of our international conferences in Costa Rica, we had a group present. After one of the evening services, the person in charge of the group came up to me and told me they were starving and needed to get some food right away. At 10:30 p.m., fast food was the only choice. So, I went to the fast food place in my car they came in the bus. There were about forty people in this group, so little things became big things very quickly. Additionally, there were fifteen more who were with us from Honduras. When we showed up just before closing time, I don't think the staff of the place was very happy. I told them I would help them with their orders. I had imagined that a group member would step and say, "Combo number one," and I would translate, "We need 'combo uno.'" Or even better, maybe four or five in the group would say, "We all want combo number...whatever." Well, it didn't go that way. The first person said they would like a combo number one with no

ketchup and extra onions. The next person would order another combo with extra this and none of that. I even had some ask for the Coca-Cola in a bottle, not in a glass. Doing this forty times was exhausting. I went home and told Marjorie I would never help people order their food ever again; to this day, I haven't. It is just too complicated; a lot of wasted energy for nothing. Oh yes, and half the group was ill the next morning! Marjorie was sweet and motherly to them. I thought it served them right. By the way, special orders do upset the cooks at closing time, no matter what their slogan is!

If we have a group, and it's a fast food moment or even a food court situation, I just hand out money, tell them to get what they want to eat, and quietly disappear. Things have proven to flow more smoothly doing it this way.

Crepes and Waffles does not disappoint me or anyone else in the group. As a team, we find time to rest a little and enjoy a nice meal. Some decide to wander around in the local small mall and shop around for that perfect gift for their spouse back home.

Our evening graduation is located just across the street from the mall and restaurant. This is wonderful, because as you may remember, we began our day on the other side of the mountains. However, I think it would have been easier to walk than take the van. The one-way streets and private gates make the short trip seem extra-long. The ministry of helps greets us as we step out of the van. They bless us by carrying all our things and escorting us around the people. They are prepared to escort us directly on the platform, but we have graduation attire to put on first. Once we are ready, they take us inside. Everyone is ready to begin the service. Tonight will be unique in the fact that this is a graduation of ninety-four students from one congregation. The pastor of this church is Henry Castillo. He is a mover and a shaker. I truly enjoy seeing him minister to his people. He was one of the pastors I met with during the ladies' conference just a few days ago. He was telling me how the Bible Institute has helped his people. People who were unstable and undependable are now some of his most productive members. *This is a great report!*

Because of my good relationship with this pastor, I take my liberty and share a few minutes with the church and graduates before introducing the commencement speaker. As I look over the crowd, the front rows are filled with blue-robed graduates. The church has come not only for an evening service but to celebrate the graduation of their now third group of graduates from this church. The pastor rented the hall for the graduation. We are not in their normal sanctuary. He did this so there would be plenty of space for all of the people. Just one look around, and you can see the hall is already at capacity. People are standing in the back and out in the hallway peering through the double doors.

While I address the church, I invite the Pastor to stand next to me. We simply converse with each other in front of those gathered for the graduation service. It may seem an odd thing to do, but it is quite edifying. I begin by thanking him for his work and support. He, in turn, speaks of the friendship we have developed over time and about how he appreciates the Bible Institute and our involvement in his church.

**A word from
Pastor Henry Castillo**

There aren't enough words to thank our God and Mutual Faith Ministries for this wonderful Bible Institute that has brought innumerable testimonies to my congregation.

Today we are graduating more than forty people for the second year, and more than fifty people for the first year. I can still recall what a brother from our church told our congregation. He told us that he had been a Christian for a while before joining our church, but he had been called a rebel. He started believing what others told him, and he thought he was a rebel without a good future. However, the Bible Institute changed his perspective, and now he has a marvelous ministry with blessed disciples. He understood the principles of being God's shield bearer, of having a servant's heart, and all of the wonderful subjects that are in God's Word. His life has changed, and he has changed many lives. We ask our Lord to greatly bless this Ministry and the Bible Institute.

**Pastor Henry Castillo
Mision Cristiana Berakah,
Bogota, Colombia**

Next, I introduce the ministry team. They are seated on the platform at a special table prepared for them. I lean over and ask Dr. Braswell to say a few words and greet everyone before the main message is delivered by Dr. Roger Price.

I begin by saying, "Tonight, I get to be the good guy as M.L. has indicated that all students are to take one last test before being allowed to graduate this evening." I don't think anyone believed me because everyone just laughed.

Two of the students give a testimony that I am supposed to translate from Spanish to English so the team can understand. Although I did translate, I felt I did not do very well. My mind is wired to translate from English to Spanish and not the other way around.

One of the graduates testifies how the Lord has recently healed him of cancer. He said he went to a doctor when he wasn't feeling well about a year ago. After a preliminary exam and other necessary tests had been run, he was informed he had cancer and needed to begin chemotherapy immediately. He tells us how he went home and after a couple of days of preparation he made the decision to believe God. He shared how he was studying faith in the Bible Institute, and he was a person of faith. "We are a family of faith. If I go through chemotherapy, it seems I am receiving the bad report and am not in faith." He continued, "Today, my doctors have confirmed that I am totally healed!" Everyone went wild! This set the atmosphere for the entire service, and I can see it is going to be a wonderful time!

After everyone speaks and the charge is given, it is time to hand out diplomas. This will be the last graduation in Bogota for the ministry team, so we have a special gift for them. Since the first graduation two days ago up until now, the graduates have been signing the matting of a certificate expressing their thanks for the team, our distinguished guests, and their participation. Both love this unique gift.

At some graduation services, I ask for four to six ushers to assist the graduates up and down the platform steps. Not all churches have platforms that require such assistance, but tonight we will need some help. As I previously mentioned, this church has a very organized *'ministry of helps'* team, so finding ushers is not a difficult task. I explain the main reason for using the ushers is to help people get up and down from the platform safely. You see, this is not just a kind gesture to help the ladies. No, it is to help the *men!* Women are accustomed to wearing long dresses and skirts, but there is a strong possibility that the men might trip on their graduation robes! Everyone laughs, but it truly is a disaster we hope to avoid!

We hand out the diplomas to some very excited, and yes, loud graduates. After lots of photos, hugs and kisses on the cheek, we finally get to go home or to the hotel to get some sleep. Today was our first double hitter, with our second scheduled for tomorrow.

A word from Dr. Price

An amazing thing happened as I traveled on my assigned journey with God-I met Don Korach. In fact, I met Don, Margie and their children at their own home. I was one of the early visitors when the Bible Institute first began. I'll never forget their hospitality and the love we shared, both in Costa Rica as well as when they visited the Bible college in our city. It is a great honor and wonderful to be a part of helping those who have had little opportunity to study in depth. When I think of the graduations, especially in Bogotá, and the great joy of the graduates upon receiving their certificates, I am humbled at the cost they were willing to pay to receive an education.

It is incredible to know we had a small part in helping them accomplish God's purpose in their lives.

I'll never forget the time I spent with Don in Costa Rica, Nicaragua, and Colombia, interacting with students, graduates and teachers. While there is danger, as Don mentioned, I have always been impressed by the great love the Latin people have for God. The Gospel will never be stopped by tyrants or by thieves who intend harm; for the love of Jesus will override all of their efforts!

Dr. Roger Price
International President, AMT/ICBT

Day 6

Double Hitter Sunday - Who Let the Cows Out?

Today is Sunday. It is ministry team's last day of ministry, and it will be another double header with two graduations on the schedule. Once again, I find everyone on time, ready and waiting for me in the hotel lobby. I cannot ask for a better way to begin another busy day. We are on our way with only one small task along the way. We had to leave before breakfast was served at the hotel and are now in search of a nice place to eat.

Everyone is a bit tired, so it will be a quiet two-hour ride to our first graduation service. We head out the northern side of Bogota; this time toward the city of Chiquinquirá in the department of Boyacá. Chiquinquirá is located 8,432 feet above sea level, which is only 229 feet lower than Bogota. However, it is a very cool place with average yearly temperatures of only fifty-eight degrees Fahrenheit.

As the sun rises, it brings light to one of the dairy regions in the country. There are rolling hills and pastures filled with Holstein and Jersey cows. As the fog lifts over the lakes and rivers, it discloses a picturesque view of the valleys below. This view is incredible, but changes in only minutes as the sun burns away the fog. I want to wake the rest of the team so they too can enjoy the breathtaking view. After all, in just a few moments the fog will be gone, and the view will be altogether different. I decide against it thinking they might prefer resting as much as possible before breakfast.

As I lean back and take in the beauty of the countryside, my mind begins to wander.

I remember our first Correspondence School. The ministry had already obtained the curriculum, which had been adopted from Guatemala. All of the details had been worked out, and we could see how easy it would be to implement. However, we did not know that was the only easy part. The challenge before us was narrowed to a couple of questions: How do you acquire students for a correspondence school? And, what is the best way to get the word out?

Although a few pastors had used this curriculum in their churches, the number of students we might obtain from that particular source was only a handful. Our vision was not only to have dozens of correspondence students but to have hundreds, and why not even thousands? We knew potential students were out there, but how would we find them? It was the Catholic Church that would solve our problem and provide a solution.

You see, Costa Rica has a patron saint, and each year hundreds of thousands of Catholics make a pilgrimage to the church of their patron saint. In fact, the roads from San Jose to

Cartago become so jammed with people that the streets on that route are off limits to automobile traffic.

One such pilgrimage to the Catholic Church was scheduled in our area on August 2nd, and our correspondence school was to open in September. The masses of people would be passing very close to our ministry center. This proved to be a God-provided, tailor-made advertising opportunity. We decided to feed the hungry pilgrims.

We worked with local churches that took turns providing free coffee and food to those who walked by and at the same time handed out tracts about the upcoming launch of the correspondence school. Within a couple of hours, we had handed out thousands and thousands of tracts.

The tract we used was specifically designed to minister to Roman Catholics. It was very well done and was the perfect tool to reach this particular group of people. The tract begins with Mary at the wedding feast in Cana of Galilee. She is speaking to the servants, telling them to do whatever Jesus told them to do, and from that point forward Jesus preaches the Gospel message. The tract then announced our upcoming correspondence school in detail.

You can imagine the response! By early September, we received hundreds of letters from people interested in knowing more about Jesus and also interested in the correspondence school!

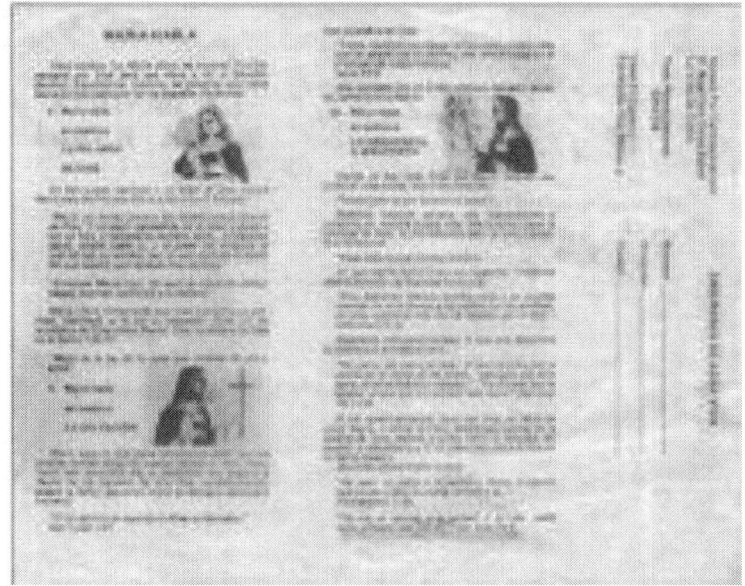

    The group begins to stir, so I ask the driver to find a place to have breakfast. It only takes a few turns before we stumble on a small location. It is unusual to see children standing outside flagging travelers down and inviting them to come inside for a home cooked meal. We later learn that the cook just happens to be the mother of the children who waved us into the little business. Although this method of bringing in business is very unconventional, it was exactly what we were looking for at the moment.

    We enjoy a nice breakfast, and everyone eats what they want. A couple of us have breakfast arepas, which is very Colombian. Most have fried or scrambled eggs with bacon and a tortilla, and one even has steak and eggs. It doesn't get much better than that!

    We are now over halfway into our morning trip, and in less than an hour, we will be at our first graduation service for the day.

    Chiquinquirá is a small city, and for several reasons, it reminds me of Cartago back in Costa Rica. It is considered to be the religious capital of Colombia. It is the home to the Basílica de Chiquinquirá, which is the home of the image of the Virgin de Chiquinquirá, the patroness saint of Colombia.

    A religious city in Latin America means a couple of things: It is a Roman Catholic city that holds a pilgrimage once a year so that the 'faithful' can express their commitment to their patron saint, and it is a city with religious overtones that will affect all churches and denominations. I am especially moved by the fact that we have friends in this city who work with the Bible Institute. Working in such a place is challenging due to religious oppression, and I am encouraged to know that we can offer them on-going assistance.

Guess what city in Costa Rica has the highest percentage of alcoholism? You might think it to be the capital or maybe even one the coastal party towns, but you would be correct only if you guessed Cartago. Religion is a heavy burden for the people, and some escape its weightiness through alcohol. This often develops into alcoholism. I imagine it is the same in Chiquinquirá.

We drive straight to the church, but this is no easy task since this incredibly old city is built on the side of a mountain with narrow, winding one-way streets. One wrong turn and we could be totally lost! Thank God our driver isn't too shy to ask for directions.

This is our second graduation for this church. Another church has sent their graduates so they will all graduate together. Both the pastor and his wife will be graduating with us, which makes this an extraordinary occasion! I consider a pastor who hosts the Bible Institute in their church a wise pastor, but one who is willing to study along with his students stands out above the others!

As we enter the church, I am reminded that Dr. Price was in this church on his last visit a few years ago. Of course, he recognized the church and the pastor, as this pastor stands out. He is easy to remember; certainly not because he is the tallest person you have ever met--nor is his wife! They are memorable because they are the friendliest people you could ever meet and are always smiling! They have two little girls, and the ministry is a family affair for them. At the last graduation, the pastor and his wife led praise and worship. The girls danced with the dance team and were so cute they stole the show!

The preliminary protocol is complete in just a few minutes. The graduates are ready to begin the service. In fact, they are ready by the time I get my graduation robe on. As the music begins, I am happy to see the pastor and his wife will lead the worship service again, but this time they are joined by two other members of the music team. The bonus? They all have on graduation robes! It is an extraordinary occasion!

The graduation is part of the regular Sunday morning service, and the entire church is excited about its students and graduates. There is a total of twenty-three people from two different churches graduating, and we all have a wonderful time! However, we discover we have graduation gowns but have forgotten the caps!

Forgetting the graduation caps means there will be no *'cap toss'* ceremony. This was a bit disappointing for everyone, but remember what I told you about improvising in the ministry? Our improvisation on this day makes this yet again a one of a kind graduation ceremony. While we forgot the caps, we have another important piece of the ceremony. There is a scarf with the Bible Institute logo, which is very nice. I have a few myself. They are imprinted with not only the Bible Institute logo, but the date of the graduation and other bits of information.

No, we do not have caps to toss in the air, but we can surely let the scarves fly! So, ready for the countdown: "One, two and three! Hallelujah!" It is interesting to see what appears to be balls of material flying up in the air and curly streamer like objects floating down.

After the service, refreshments are served to everyone. I noticed the cake as I went back to change before the service. When I first saw it, I noticed it was decorated with what appeared to be artificial gold fruit. It looked quite nice! As I am given a piece of the cake, I immediately notice the small piece of plastic fruit on my portion. As I look closer, I realize the fruit was not artificial. It was very real. It has simply been painted gold! I must admit; it is fun eating *gold colored grapes*, and I can tell everyone else enjoys the cake as well. Before leaving for our next meeting, we have one last thing to do; have our pictures taken with the graduates.

It is still early as we make our way to the city of Tunja. Chiquinquirá is a city in the department of Boyacá. We are now going the capital of Boyacá; a city called Tunja. The history of the city of Tunja is interesting. It was founded on August 6, 1539, by a Spanish captain named Gonzalo Suarez Rendon. It is difficult to imagine we are going to a city that existed two hundred thirty-seven years *before* the American Revolution!

As I think about the Spaniards there so many years ago, I am reminded of driving into Panama from Costa Rica, and I begin to chuckle to myself.

As you might imagine, I have an accent when I speak Spanish, but I do not normally have a recognizable accent. Why? My learning the language has been influenced by so many different people and places that I often find people can't quite figure out where I'm from.

When you cross borders, there are always children or young people willing to assist you as you walk through the necessary steps, and they want nothing more than a tip. I have been across these borders enough that I do not often need help, but this time I had arrived at the border and had forgotten to make the necessary photocopies. Since I didn't want to look for a place to have copies made, I found myself with a new friend.

Before I knew it, my new friend arrived with the needed copies, but for some reason one of the officials had stepped out. We were going to have to wait about a half an hour for his return. It seemed like a great time for a cup of coffee as we waited at the border. While waiting, my new friend began to ask about my accent. It was obvious to him that Elmer, a Costa Rican who was traveling with me on this trip, was from Costa Rica. Elmer has heard discussions of this nature many times. Sometimes people think I sound Portuguese, French or even German. Seldom does anyone say I sound like I am from the United States of America. My friends and colleagues recognize my American accent, but those who don't know me rarely guess correctly.

Elmer continues conversing with our new friend. He tells us he hears different accents all day long, and that he is very good at guessing where people are from. He is certain he can tell where I am from--to him it is obvious. I am from Spain! He is, of course, incorrect, but not wanting to disappoint him Elmer says, "You are good!" Soon after, we finished at the border and continued our trip.

It will take about an hour to travel the winding mountain separating Chiquinquirá and Tunja. There is a nice colonial town along the way. It is a nice place to stop and stretch your legs and also a great place to shop for Colombian souvenirs.

We arrive in Tunja just in time for the scheduled lunch meeting. The meeting includes local pastors who have already incorporated the Bible Institute in their churches, as well as those interested in doing so. I always enjoy these types of meetings. It is a chance for pastors who know the benefits and blessings of incorporating the Bible Institute to share with new pastors who are interested. Those who are using the Bible Institute always have a few questions, but they are also the best promoters of the program. These pastors have discovered an important and productive training tool for making disciples. No wonder they unselfishly want to share it with others; especially their pastor friends!

We have a great time of fellowship as they share and ask questions about the Bible Institute. We are privileged to sit and listen to some of the dreams and visions for their local churches. All of the pastors are invited and will attend our next graduation. One of the pastors shares about our syllabus, which addresses the need of prayer. The pastor wants me to know how this syllabus has helped and truly impacted his church. It is during our conversation that I share an interesting fact about this syllabus.

Sometimes people want to know what material, subject or commentary was first translated into Spanish for the Bible Institute. They often assume the first translated was the first commentary we teach, but this was not the case. The first theme we translated was called, "The Need of Prayer." The response we often get is, "Oh. That is nice. We can all agree that prayer is important." Now, I believe in prayer as much or more than the next person. It would be impossible to live for years on the foreign field without a personal, prayerful relationship with the One who called us to the field, but the main reason we chose this material to translate first was its size. After reviewing the available commentaries, we simply chose the smallest one. It was a great commentary to cut our 'translating teeth' on.

As we leave the restaurant to make our way to the graduation, I see a sign that reminds of some of Tunja's history.

It was the capital city of a short-lived country called *United Provinces of New Granada.* This country, one I'm sure you've never heard about, only existed for six years; from 1810 to 1816. It then became an important region of Colombia. Today, Tunja is a college town with twenty percent of the population attending a college or university. The residents of Tunja are quick to tell any visitor that they live in the departmental capital that has the highest altitude in all of Colombia. The pastors there tease as they tell us the anointing of God flows from the top down! *I love their humor!*

A pastor tells us something else that catches my attention. As we know, Colombia has been a war zone for what seems forever. If not the drug lords fighting, it is guerrillas, but today we learn that Tunja has never been touched by the war. *Never been touched by the war? Unbelievable!* The reason is due to the city's location and the type of vegetation that grows on the mountain. It grows wonderful grass for cows, but short vegetation makes for terrible hiding places. If you cannot hide, you cannot fight! So, finding this quiet, peaceful place in this war-torn nation is amazing, and maybe he is right; maybe the anointing *does* flow from the top!

The Bible Institute will have thirty-six graduates from two different churches in Tunja today. It will be the last ministry activity for this group. They have done a remarkable job and working with them has been a joy.

By now you know the drill--papers signed, clothes changed, the official charge given by our special speaker and our graduates get to toss their caps into the air. Afterward, pictures are taken, and another graduation is complete. This is the team's sixth graduation in only a few days, but it is the one and only graduation of importance to these students. It is a proud, celebratory event for the graduating students, and although we are all tired, we want them to know we are proud of them as well.

This particular graduation is quite special. Perhaps it is the realization this is the last opportunity to minister together in Colombia. All five members wanted to share, and whether it was a word, a song, or someone blowing the shofar for the students, it was a memorable time.

We have a long ride to the hotel. I know everyone is tired of the travel time in an uncomfortable van, but we will rest tonight. We all recognize it has been a productive week of ministry for the Kingdom of God. The ministry team has had a blessed time touching lives in Colombia and of course, the Colombians have touched their lives as well!

A Word from
Dr. Verda Thompson
SIGNIFICANT REFLECTIONS (Costa Rica)
Moving Forward With Purpose
A New Ministry

In the fall of 1990, we, the American Mission Teams and a Bible College, began in California. Then, as an infant ministry, we moved to Norris City, Illinois.

Crossroads Bible Church, pastored by Dr. Leo Hall welcomed us. We began classes in Norris City, IL, Paducah, KY and Sikeston, MO. We taught once a week at each location and after three years it became evident that Norris City would be our home location. A group of about forty believers began to help develop courses and student enrollment grew.

In 1993, we had the opportunity to open a College site in Kiev, Ukraine. Soon people were translating the material into Russian. In 1996, three AMT pastors were invited to Malawi, Africa, and a Bible College was born there. During these formative years, college sites opened in Kentucky and Virginia.

Then came an open door to Central and South America through Drs. David and Harriet Craig from Sikeston, MO. They told us of a young minister from Costa Rica, who was interested in the material. They asked if we would give the course material to him for translation into Spanish.

That began our relationship with Mutual Faith Ministries and Rev. Don Korach. So in December of 1996 the material went to Costa Rica. The first school opened in May 1997.

Brother Korach worked with believers to get the material translated, even finding proofreaders at the University in Costa Rica.

Soon an explosion took place and in the last eighteen years colleges have opened under Mutual Faith in several Central and South America Countries. We praise The Lord for the open doors and godly connections!

Now For Some Funny and Fond Memories...

American Mission Teams – International College of Bible Theology began to send mission students and teachers to visit the Korach's in Costa Rica. Here are a few memorable notes:

We sent Brother Greg Hughes to minister, visit school sites and hold graduation in Nicaragua. All was going well when the group had an encounter with a dog. The dog bit Rev. Don Korach! Praise The Lord he was okay, and it wasn't Brother Greg!

Then we had the Eternal Group. They were a group of six ministers all wanting to minister and teach every day. Rev. Don was challenged to say the least. To add to it, this group stayed two weeks. Brother Don told me never again—never that many for that long!

Let's not forget we had a group go to Colombia to help with graduations and a women's meeting. There were Bishop Eddy, Dr. Roger and a couple of others including two women ministers, Pastor Donna, and Deborah. The meetings went well. However, at the large graduations, there were no gowns for the two women. The ladies let me know about it when they returned from Colombia! That year Brother Don called it the "Graduation Bonanza!"

So we have had a biting dog, an eternal group, and missing gowns. Now for the trips I've made! On a trip to Costa Rica with Pastor Sally, we stayed with Brother Don and Sister Margie and their two children. We had a great time ministering, visiting prisons, shopping, and sightseeing. Bishop Eddy was with us. He stayed at another place, but we traveled and ministered together.

On one trip, we honored Rev. Don with an Honorary Doctorate and his earned Master Degree. Dr. Don received some gifts. Among these gifts was a bottle of spirits. Well, we went back to the Korach's and Don, Sally, and I had a bit of a party. We had cheese, crackers and a sip or two. Not much touched our lips, but we made a lot of noise laughing. Margie, Don's wife, thought we were living it up. The next morning we tried to convince her different, but I don't think she believed it.

The trip to Colombia, holding three large graduations and looking for restrooms along the way reminded me of trips into the Ukraine countryside. Relief stations were few and very far between. On one of the trips, we went to the Spider-Man movie and the next day six of the seven of us were sick with the flu. I was pretty much ok, and we flew home. Pastor Sally was sick all the way home on the plane.

Now, for two more poignant recollections. Oh, the wonderful technology of the fax machine. It certainly helps with communication. However, let me tell you about the frustrating fax, or shall we say the conflicting fax. Fairly early on in our networking relationship with Mutual Faith, we sent fax messages. One day I faxed Rev. Don a letter complimenting him on the schools, students and translation of the material into Spanish. He soon fired back a fax and said, "Complaint? What complaint?" He had misread the fax! We quickly got that straightened out and have laughed about it many times over the years.

Last but certainly not least is "My Dear." One would have to know me to understand that I seldom greet people with endearing greetings such a Dear. However, I grew so fond of Don and his family that I started calling him Dear; being the upfront person that I am, Don decided I must really care about him to call him Dear.

In conclusion, I and the ministry love Don, Margie and their children, Rachel and Donald. I thank them for their wonderful hospitality and praise the Lord for the work they do. It is a privilege to labor together in The Master's Vineyard.

Well, Dear, I hope you can use some of my information. We at AMT-ICBT are so grateful that you had the material translated years ago. Thousands of people have been blessed by it. It is on many school sites and in prisons in Mexico. We also have several schools sites in the U.S. that use the Spanish curriculum.

Love you all,
Dr. Verda Thompson, Sister Verda, Dr. T

Day 7

Team Goes Home –
Time for a Big Roller Coaster Ride!

I arrive at the hotel with a little extra time to spare. No rushing around or running late this morning. I find everyone going through the checkout procedures.

Checkout at the hotels can be challenging at times. Some hotels have great service while others do not quite meet the standard. It is surprising to see how concerned some hotel staff are with the mini-bar in the rooms. I cannot help but wonder why they would send someone to do inventory once you have already checked out. It seems it would be quite easy to charge for a missing bottle of water or a candy bar even after checkout, especially since they have all the credit card information on file.

It can create a brief moment of celebration when checkout time finally concludes!

Once I had a group of thirty with me in Cali, Colombia. I knew the situation with the mini-bar inventory could become a huge issue when we all tried to leave at the same time. I talked to the manager about my concern, and she was very helpful. She said, "No problem. We can pull the mini-bar early."

What a great idea! I wanted to double check, so I proceeded to ask, "You can do that?" She assured me they could, and, in fact, had pulled the bars twenty-four hours prior to checkout. What a blessing and a timesaver that was! Now, I would not have to deal with a candy bar and liquor count so early in the morning!

Today is a travel day. The ministry team will be heading back to the states. They have worked together so well this week. They will now go back to their homes in various cities and states, but their time together in Bogota will always be an irreplaceable memory. Once everyone is checked in at the airport, it will be time for me to leave as well. I will leave Bogota and head to my next assignment. Traveling does have its moments. Immediately my thoughts take me back to the time when I was driving from San Jose, Costa Rica to Panama City, Panama.

Crossing borders is always interesting and/or challenging, but Panama has an added challenge to deal with on every trip. I usually have little or no trouble crossing borders from one country to another. Only in Panama have I experienced more than one frustrating checkpoint along the

way. Approximately thirty minutes into the country, we had to stop at checkpoint number one. Elmer was driving. However, we were both confused as to whether he should stop or not. There was a stop sign there, but the police, who were dressed military style, just ignored us as we traveled down the road. In other countries, it is customary to slow down while awaiting a signal from the police as to what they want you to do. They will either wave you on or point you to a parking place, but that was not the case that day. Elmer was driving very slow but had continued steadily in the lane without stopping. When they realized what was happening, they jumped into action. We were instructed to move out of the drive through lane and into the lane where we were to park. The tirade that followed included questions and comments regarding our driving abilities and something about Jack in the Box! After checking our two-mile old paperwork, he reminded us that he was in charge. He eventually allowed us to continue our trip. The atmosphere was so thick you could cut it with a knife. To lighten things up a bit, I teased and said, "Elmer, I told you to stop! What is your problem?" He looked at me and replied, "No, you didn't!" At that point, we both burst into laughter as we continued our journey.*

After months of preparation and multiple trips to Panama, it was time to hold the long-awaited conference. It will be a week and a half of 24/7 ministry activities. A group of twenty-five will be with us, plus the VIPs, Live TV Time, Studio Time and Graduations from the Bible Institute. Then there is the conference itself! However, before we can do anything, we first have to get to Panama City!

After saying farewell at home, we still had a couple of stops in San Jose. First, we had to go to the office and pick up *a few last minute items. The van was packed. It was filled with equipment, materials, and clothing. Our next stop was the bank. We had to take money with us. The conference expense money had been transferred into a separate account, and we needed to make a withdrawal in order to take the money with us into Panama. One of the bank administrators is a believer and a friend of mine. He happily assisted me in processing the $15,000 cash withdrawal.*

With our stops complete, it was time to head for the border. It was 3:00 p.m., which meant we should be at the border by 8:00 p.m. and across the border into Panama before they closed at 10:00 p.m. As we were heading out of San Jose, we decided to stop at the last McDonald's. We made a short trip through the drive-thru, ordering our food through one of those crazy squawk boxes. We paid the lady at the window and drove to the next window. Great! We are now on our way. We had traveled down the road about fifteen minutes when I told Elmer I was ready to eat. That is when it hit us; we had driven in and through but never stopped to pick up our food. Talk about being distracted!

Needless to say, we turned back and drove up to the window. We confessed; yes, we were the ones who ordered and paid for our food over thirty minutes earlier and just drove off leaving it behind. It took them only a few minutes to fill our order with fresh items. Although, I am sure it would have taken less time if there hadn't been so much laughter going on! I know we were the laughing stock of the entire McDonald's crew, and honestly, it was funny!

Somehow, we made it to the border in record time, but once at the Panamanian border we had to take care of all the preliminaries with Customs. We needed to list everything that needed to be declared. I usually do not have anything to list on the declaration. However, this trip was different. We had

$15,000 in cash with us, and we had no idea what they would have us do. We explained the purpose of our trip into the country. We also explained how the money would be used.

One of the men at Customs had heard about the conference via the television advertising. He was a believer, and his words were totally unexpected. He said, "Don't do anything! Don't you know the Customs Department is corrupt? If they know you have that kind of money with you, they will call a friend, and you won't make it to Panama City." Then he went on to tell us stories of people who hadn't made it from the airport to the hotel before getting robbed at gunpoint. Then he asked us to give him a ride. At this point, it would have been difficult to say no.

As we drove on, checkpoint number one came into sight, and we knew we would have to stop. As we stopped, one of the men there saw the gentleman from Customs with us, so he just waved us on. A little past the checkpoint, we dropped our passenger off. It was late, and we were tired, so we spent the night in the city of David. David is the first big city for us as we enter northern Panama, and I have stayed there many times. It is the first city in Panama where I ministered many years ago.

It is about another seven hours of drive time to Panama City from the city of David. Approximately an hour from there, we will find checkpoint number two where Laurel and Hardy work. It seems Laurel and Hardy's job is to bother every foreigner in a vehicle from out of the country.

We had separated the money so that $8,000.00 was in my bag and $7,000.00 in Elmer's bag. Of course, you probably guessed it; Laurel and Hardy pulled us over for inspection. Our paperwork was in order, but they decided to open all our bags. Oh, how I wished that the brother we had met at the border would have been with us that day. There was nothing to hide. We had only our equipment, materials, the bags with our *belongings and the money. Boy did the guards get excited! We were told to move the vehicle completely out of the way in order not to block traffic.*

Of course, they asked us about the money and what we were doing with it. I told them exactly how much was there, but they did not believe me. They started counting it bill by bill, all in stacks of twenty dollar bills. They counted, counted and recounted. The more the men counted, the more confused they became. Finally, they gave up and decided that they believed me. He then told me he would have to call the border for further instructions. We were there for over an hour dealing with the unnecessary hassle, when one of the officers finally says, "It looks like everything is in order. I guess you can move on."

Our nerves were a bit frayed by this time, and this is where my assertive side took control. I said, "Okay. You now have all of our information, right? Now, I need something from you. I need your name and your work ID number." They were accustomed to giving the orders all day; telling people to stop or not to stop and ordering people to show what they were transporting. The officer was obviously not happy with my requiring information from them. To their credit, I was given the information I requested, which I then handed it to Elmer so that he could write it on the back of the paperwork. I admit, I could have used a nicer tone. Elmer looked at me and said, "Relax! We are almost finished!"

Once we were back on the road after the checkpoint, I explained to Elmer why I did what I did. "Elmer. These two guys are the only people besides ourselves that know we have this money with us. They know who we are, where we are going and even when we are going to be there. If anything happens, I want their fingerprints all over our travel plans!"

Thankfully, we made it the rest of the way without incident. The conference and the entire week of ministry were excellent!

The van is already parked in front of the hotel along with two other vehicles that will transport the luggage to the airport. It only takes a few minutes to load the vehicles. It is a quick ride to the airport with such sparse traffic so early in the morning. This will be our last time in the van together. As everyone gets situated in the van, they begin to share about the wonderful time they've had in Colombia. The atmosphere is filled with excitement as each one shares what they liked best. I always like to hear about the likes and dislikes of a ministry team's experiences during a visit.

I escort the group as they check-in and acquire their boarding passes. A problem free experience at the airport is always a plus for everyone involved. Part of the group wants to go directly to the Immigration checkpoint and head to the gate right away. Others want to find a cup of coffee and breakfast before going through Immigration. I stay to have one last cup of coffee with the remaining part of the team before directing them to the Immigration checkpoint. After our final handshakes, hugs and goodbyes they make their way through Immigration. They will certainly have much to talk about when they get home. They will have many things to share with their church and others about ministering in Colombia.

The ministry team's departure is always one of mixed emotions as our lives become knit together in a special way during their stay. They came and not only saw what we were doing in the ministry but became a part of the ministry itself. They were extremely helpful.

Since I grew up on a resort in central Minnesota, I was accustomed to meeting all kinds of people from all over the map. People spent their vacations with us; some staying only through the weekend, but some as long as a couple of weeks. Sometimes large families would rent the entire facility. When I say families--I mean large families! It was a great place to see the very best of people.

In the reception area at the resort, there was a little sign not much larger than a postcard that read, *All of our guests bring happiness; some by coming and others by going.* The team that is leaving Colombia will definitely be remembered as a happiness *by coming* group of guests!

When the last members of the group make their way past Immigration, I head back to the check-in counter area. A few minutes later M.L. arrives to meet with me. We are going to the city of Florencia this morning to continue with the *"Graduation Bonanza!"* This group has gone home, but I am not yet half finished. Six graduations are complete with seven more to go!

Florencia is on the southeastern side of Colombia. It was founded in 1908 by Roman Catholic missionary. This made me think of the movie from the 80's "The Mission" with Robert De Niro. Florencia is the capital city of the department of Caquetá. It is located in the middle of farmland and surrounded by beef cattle farms and rice fields. It serves as a trade center for those living in the densely forested lowland that stretches to the South and East.

We encounter problems getting checked-in initially. The airline computer is down. *How does one get any work done without a computer?* I am impressed with the way the lady solved the problem. She pulled out a boarding pass and a pen and simply *wrote* our information on it manually. I have not seen handwritten *anything* in an airport for years! I am not even sure it will be acceptable! However, I am assured there will be no problem.

I do not have to deal with Immigration as I am not leaving the country. Still, I will encounter security. There will be three different people checking me and my things. They do not trust each other, so everyone has to do a thorough job of checking. First, the army takes their turn. This can often begin outside on the sidewalk. Next, the local police take their turn. Last but not least, there is the airport's security. All of this is done by hand. There is no technology used to search or scan. Yes, the entire process is done by hand as you and your luggage are searched and searched and searched again!

Once we complete the check-in process, we proceed to the regional flight gates. Looking out of the window, we realize the trip will not be in one of the large jets but one of the little planes hidden in the back. Our flight is a little late, but it isn't long before we are all seated. The plane begins to taxi on the tarmac in preparation for takeoff. The flight out of Bogota is impressive. The city stretches beautifully in all directions. It is nearly impossible to see the entire city at once. Our flight is an interesting one as we fly up and over the mountains first. We then fly back down on the other side. The view is spectacular as we fly over immense forests spread out as far as the eye can see. It feels like an enormous rollercoaster; click, click, click, up, up, up and then, *swoosh* down we go!

Gazing out the window, I remember the first time we considered organizing an extension school. The concept was unfamiliar to the team at first, but they were willing to give it a try.

My thoughts take me to the extension school in Puerto Jimenez. When we were still in the initial set-up stage, I learned that getting to Puerto Jimenez was only half the fun of establishing a school at that location. Since I live in San Jose, I had to take a taxi at 4:30 a.m. to get to the airline office in San Jose before I could even think of traveling to Puerto Jimenez. I was transported to the airport from there by bus to board a plane. It would be a short domestic flight that would take me to (GLF) Golfito. Golfito is not far from my final destination, Puerto Jimenez. This flight takes approximately thirty-five minutes. When compared to a ten-hour road trip, it is definitely the time-saving way to go. I have boarded many types of planes for this flight over the years. One plane that stands out in my mind is the DC3. As you board this plane, the tail is lower than the front of the plane. You walk down hill to your seat. The first time I flew in one of these planes, I couldn't help but think, "This plane is so old my Grandfather could have flown on it!"

On another flight, I remember we had to board a very small plane. I guess the gentleman sitting next to me could tell by my facial expressions that I was not happy about being transported on this aircraft. He leaned over and said, "We are flying a great plane! Do you know that if we have any trouble, it can land anywhere?" His words of encouragement did not bring me comfort.

On one occasion, I missed my return flight. I knew the schedule. I knew what time I needed to be at the airstrip, but on that particular day I just did not make it there on time. I do not remember if I lost track of time while talking to the students, or perhaps it was because I was enjoying myself so much in class and time got away from me, but my flight out was gone. Fortunately, this was not a problem. I knew the flight schedules and knew there would be one last flight back to San Jose that day.

As we waited patiently for that last flight out, we were informed there would be no more flights that day. In fact, there would be no more flights in the foreseeable future. Of course, I was quite unhappy about this because it meant a ten to twelve-hour bus ride if I wanted to get back home. As I was processing my disappointment, the news came about the plane I should have been on for the earlier flight. This was the flight time I normally took and the flight I should have been on, but wasn't. They reported that the flight had crashed into the side of a mountain! There were no survivors! Strangely enough, that bus ride home didn't feel so long after all, and I assure you, it is one I will always be most thankful for!

Florencia is only four hundred and forty-nine feet above sea level. The moment the door of the plane is opened, you feel the tropical heat rush inside. As I walk to the terminal, a few things catch my eye. The military helicopters sitting off to the left seem to be the main focus of many of the soldiers as they work to clean them. It seems their goal is to make them shine inside and out.

Off to the right side, I notice some crop dusting planes. I will not discover what they were spraying until day eight of my trip. You will learn about that tomorrow. Personally, seeing the presence of the military is always comforting. If the military is present in the area, I assume the odds are in my favor that the area is secure.

I had planned to come to Florencia almost two years ago. We have students there, and I wanted to encourage them. It seemed at that time that the best way to do this was to come in person and celebrate their graduation with them. My original plan was to fly in and hold the graduation ceremony at the airport, then return to Bogota the same day. You see, this gets complicated in an area of the country that has so much turmoil.

Two years ago, when I agreed to go, I could not have gone. It was not a secure part of the country. This city, known as the gate to the Amazon, was heavily influenced by the drug cartel. It was also influenced by the guerrillas of Colombia, known as the FARC--Revolutionary Armed Forces of Colombia.

Our students and pastor friends in the Bible Institute have paid a price to be here. The guerrillas have ransacked their homes and churches, as well as threatened to kidnap them and their children. The guerrilla soldiers have gone into meetings to see who is studying and what they are studying. The Ministry had to change our printing format, so as not to place our friends in any more danger. We took all references to the United States out of the material.

It only takes us a few minutes to get out of the terminal. The biggest delay is the dogs. It takes a while to smell all of the luggage and passengers. The pastor, who I had seen in Bogota, greets us at the door and leads us to his car. A couple of other brothers from the church, who are also our students, meet us. They are riding motorcycles. We do not have the graduation service at the airport as I had originally requested, and I can tell you that the drive from the airport to the hotel is exactly seven minutes.

The pastor is very excited because they have all finished their studies and also because we are having the graduation in his city. This reality is something that was only a dream a few months ago.

There is a meeting in the hotel where pastors and their wives have come to meet me and to discuss the Bible Institute that is held in their local churches. The hotel has everything prepared. We all sit around a long table. It is great to hear from all the pastors. They are excited to have the Bible Institute in their churches, and they are anxious to see what the day will bring.

Once we finish our quick lunch, it is time for me to get together with the teachers. One of my passions is to teach teachers. This is the perfect time and place for me to get to work. With the visiting team members now on their way home, it is time for me to shift gears and move in another direction. It is of utmost importance to this ministry. I never considered bringing the group here, only because I want to be able to keep a low profile. Traveling around with a group is not the best way to sneak in and out without being noticed.

The pastors and I go straight to the meeting room where we are joined by the other teachers who are already waiting for us. Materials are available for everyone. Once M.L. gets everything and everyone situated, it is time to get started.

It is great to hear where everyone is from and to hear what subjects they have taught. We will only have two hours together before the graduation service, but this will be quality time for sure. It is hot and uncomfortable, but no one seems to mind. They came with ears to hear and hearts to receive, and I am having a wonderful time with them all. Before I know it, it is time to wrap up my session in order for everyone to get ready for the graduation ceremony. They all have graduation robes made for the occasion. Of course, we still have lots to do as we gather signatures and meet protocol for the graduation of this great group of people.

As we begin the graduation service, a few things catch my attention. First, the graduates all look wonderful in their new robes! Their faces glow as they smile from ear to ear. Second, I look at the family and friends of the graduates. The meeting room is filled with guests and even more spill out along the poolside. It is amazing to be a part of these graduations and observe the emotions of both graduates and their families. How wonderful to make time to honor them for this major accomplishment in their lives! Graduations are truly a highlight anywhere we go. However, to hold the graduation ceremony here, in the city of Florencia is extremely special. The third thing I notice is my watch. I have one hour to minister and hand out diplomas to the fifty-seven graduates from three different churches.

When M.L. and I hand out the last diploma and close the service in prayer, the pastor who picked us up at the airport is waiting. He introduces us to his father and taps his watch with his finger reminding me of the time. He then says, "Dad is going to take you the airport. I will meet you there in a few minutes." Almost instantly our belongings arrive and are placed in the trunk via a couple of graduates. As we drive to the airport, the pastor's father thanks us for what the ministry is doing in his life and that of his son. He is very grateful for all the activities of the day.

I have always wondered why we had left the graduation in a different car and with a different driver that day. Could it have been a security issue, or was it for convenience?

I feel more secure once I arrive at the airport. Thankfully, we arrive quickly, since the airport is only seven minutes away. I am aware that airports can be targeted, but this one is fortified. I go to the counter to check in without incident. By the time I complete the check-in process, the pastor arrives. The three of us sit down to drink a cool, soft drink together and talk. The Pastor asks me if I liked the hotel accommodations. I let him know that the facility was very suitable for our time of teaching and the graduation service. He also lets me know that although I had asked that the graduation be held at the airport, it was impossible. They were unable to get the army to sign off for permission to do so. I tell him I had been made aware of the situation and had almost canceled my visit. He mentions the hotel they rented is the most secure place they could find. It is definitely more secure than their churches since it is located directly in front of the police station.

    I thank him for his help and for the wonderful time with his people. The plane has arrived, so, it is time to see some dogs and get back on the little plane headed to (BOG) Bogota.

Day 8

The Gospel in the Wild West!

This morning is my last morning in Bogota, and it is time to say farewell to Pastor J.J. and his wife. I will not be returning to Bogota on this trip except for a short layover during a flight change. My thoughts take me back to my very first visit to Bogota many years ago.

We entered Colombia through Bogota on our way to the city of Armenia. This is where we would initiate the Bible Institute in Colombia. We were blessed by people whom we never expected to be such a tremendous help to the ministry. We were only testing the waters on this initial trip and had very few contacts. Our contact in Bogota was a college student; a friend of the pastor from Armenia. We hoped to meet a few pastors and share our vision and then wait to see what might develop.

During the planning of the trip, I received a message that someone had heard of our coming and wanted to bless us with transportation. The details were a bit vague, but I was happy someone wanted to help.

When we arrived in Bogota, the college student was waiting for us at the airport with a small and I mean extremely small car. We squeezed ourselves into the little vehicle and drove all around the city for two days. A time or two we were forced to get out of the car because it would not make it up the hill with us inside. Everyone got out of the car except for the driver, and we could not help but laugh. Just imagine watching four North Americans getting out of a tiny car, at the bottom of a hill in the middle of Bogota, just to stand and observe the tiny car struggling to reach the top of the hill, with tires squealing and smoke bellowing the entire way! We would then walk up the hill and pile back into the car. It was like watching a circus!

The most interesting part of all this is that it was a group of nuns that heard about the ministry and our visit. They were the ones who wanted to bless us with transportation while we were in town. Before our arrival, they had planned to loan us their van during our visit, but when we arrived, they realized they had prior commitments and needed the van. Rather than leave us without transportation, they gathered the money to rent that little car. I felt so blessed that they were led to help us in this way. A little hill climbing was fun for both the onlookers and us.

A word from
Pastor David Craig

I have traveled in several nations, but I have never felt as secure with anyone as I have with Don Korach traveling Central and South America. Don cared for me during ten trips into Central and South America, and each trip bore good fruit that remains. God always explained the Scriptures more clearly to me while I was in the mission field. Our last mission together was in 2005, but I have many good memories of our time together. I dislike travel, but if I could translate like Philip did in Acts 8:39-40, I would continue with mission trips.

We met Don in the fall of 1983 and have worked together for many years. My wife, Harriet, introduced Don to the Bible School curriculum and the president of the college. The rest is history. Don is a keeper!

I do remember the small vehicles and especially the one the Nuns rented for our use. Many explain being in tight places as being packed 'like sardines in a can,' and that was true for our crew. Just imagine three 200 pound men squeezed into a back bench seat that is thirty inches wide. We were so tightly packed; seatbelts were unnecessary. Thankfully the highway weight scales did not require us to weigh, or we would have had to unload some passengers. We severely tested the cars clutch, but hopefully we did not destroy it.

One day we had the privilege of having a lady dentist, whose father was a military leader in the government, as our driver and guide. I was certainly glad she was driving because she knew the city. She was familiar with the area and knew how to maneuver in the insane traffic. On one occasion, we were pinched between two very large tractor-trailers as three lanes merged into one. In sheer fear of having an accident, I gasped so loudly I must have sucked all of the oxygen out of the car. She snapped, "Do you want to drive?" I immediately slid into my country boy charm and graciously declined.

In Armenia, we lived in one of the housing projects among the people to which we ministered. The lady of the house we were inhabiting was inquisitive regarding our bathing habits and freely offered us some health tips. When we requested hot water, or water above 58 degrees Fahrenheit, she informed us that hot baths would make us sick. Needless to say, we remained healthy as we followed her wisdom.

Near the end of the trip, a local business woman, Gladys Montez, took us shopping. Gladys was driving a large SUV! Man! Heaven came down, and glory filled our souls! Due to our extensive training in small vehicle packing and transportation, and our current opportunity to sit in wide leather seats, we forsook the safety of seatbelts to enjoy the freedom of individuality!

Later that evening, Gladys took me to a home meeting in a more upscale portion of the city. Oddly enough, they had hot water, and they were just as healthy as the people who bathed in cold water. Go figure!

By the Holy Ghost, I released a prophecy of a soon coming great shaking, which I thought was to be a revival. As it turned out, it was an earthquake that destroyed people, property, and the economy. In the poorer district, the people living in the three-story bamboo structures were not injured in the shaking.

Let us learn to be as flexible as the bamboo structures but immovable in our faith in God.

Harriet and I returned to Armenia the next year, and the glory of God was attracting even more people to the Kingdom of God.

**Pastor David Craig
Life Church
Sikeston Missouri**

This morning I have to be at the airport by 5:00 a.m. The computer is up and running, so before I know it, I have my boarding pass in hand with no concern I may need a handwritten boarding pass. I stop for a quick breakfast since I have already found the only open place in the airport with coffee and donuts. Before long, I am boarding one of the small aircraft on my way to the city of San Jose del Guaviare.

Wow! That is a mouth full, isn't it! I am accustomed to saying San Jose the name of our capital in Costa Rica. The city of San Jose is the capital city of the Department of Guaviare, which sits on the bank of a mighty river called the Guaviare River.

San Jose del Guaviare is located further east and south of Florencia. Since it is located on the bank of the river, it marks the area of transition from the grassland plains to the north and the tropical rainforest to the south. This tropical rainforest is the beginning of the multinational Amazon. The department of Guaviare is very isolated and has only one principle settlement, its capital San Jose. There is only one dirt road, and it is in poor condition. The road stretches to the northwest and connects Guaviare to Villavicencio. Guaviare is a fairly new department. It was officially declared on July 4, 1991, as the newest

"Political Constitution" of Colombia. Up until 1991, the area was a part of the Vaupés territory. The department of Guaviare has some special residents; the "Nukak" tribe. The Nukak tribe went undiscovered until 1988.

I review my notes as I wait for the flight. I pause and take a minute to think about my guests who were here only yesterday and are now back home. I remember my Dad's first visit to Costa Rica. It would be great to have him here with me today.

About six months after the Bowman's visit, Dad and Pastor Wendell Meyers came to stay and spent about a week. Their visit was easy in that I was able to pick them up from the airport without incident. The occasion was a significant improvement from my initial experience with visitors.

I remember Pastor Meyers asking on what subject should he preach or teach. I seldom suggest a subject or topic for someone to minister, but that time I did. There happened to be a specific particular we were teaching in the Bible School during his visit: "The Blood Covenant" so, I gave him the notes on the subject and told him to take liberty. He told me later that teaching this subject and spending time in study and preparation to teach those classes had changed his life forever.

During their visit, they ministered in the new tent in the town of Turrialba and also taught at the Bible Training Center in Puntarenas. Interestingly, since his initial visit, my Dad always finds a reason to go back to Puntarenas when he comes to Costa Rica. Puntarenas is a quaint little town on the Pacific Coast. There are perhaps nicer places to visit in Costa Rica, but for my Dad it has become a 'family tradition.' It was the first place he visited while in the country, and he has been there many times since then.

My Dad and Pastor Meyers visited to personally 'check out' the ministry. The Ministry Central Office back in the United States had instituted a policy change. The decision was made to change the amount of money missionaries were required to give the home office from their ministry contributions. Prior to that time, missionaries had voluntarily donated 10% of their income to the Ministry office. A major change occurred which required all missionaries donate a 25% 'service charge.' It was mandatory.

When my Dad heard the news about the new policy, he was quite upset. "What are these people thinking?!" he said. "You are giving of your life, and now they want to dig into your pocket." This was my dad's way of saying; Son, I am concerned about your wellbeing.

The local ministry director tried to convince my Dad of the merits of the change. He told him how wonderful this new policy would be for everyone. Of course, this man was a director, and the directors had an exemption clause that protected them from the new service charge.

Dad came to visit me with a little hope in his heart that his son had not completely lost his mind. However, he was then fully convinced of his suspicion. It was a difficult time for me, as I was between a rock and a hard place as well, due to this new procedure. The policy they had set before us was, 'pay or leave.' There was no room for discussion. I had already witnessed one family leave the mission field because of such inflexible policies.

I paid the 25% service fee for the subsequent four years, although I never told anyone about it. I was convinced that if my supporters realized I was receiving only 75% of the funds they were sending me they would not be pleased. I was concerned that they would cut me off completely. Eventually, the Ministry recognized their mistake in that matter, but it was too little too late as far as my Dad was concerned.

This plane is smaller than the one we traveled in yesterday. My carry on bag is taken to the back or *belly* of the plane due to the lack of space. The plane seems to jump off the runway in (BOG) Bogota. I suppose the smaller the plane, the quicker they can get off the ground and fly! Even though I am tired, I stay awake long enough to see the sunrise. There is something special about seeing a sunrise while in flight. The jolt of the landing at (SJE) San Jose del Guaviare wakes me, and in only a moment, someone opens the door allowing the hot, tropical air to rush inside.

Much like yesterday, upon arrival, we are greeted by dogs and their handlers. I do not see the military helicopters as before; however, I do notice the crop dusters. As we enter the terminal, a solider checks out our identification. He wants to know where I will be staying and for how long. He begins to write my responses to his questions in a large book. He then flips it over and asks me to sign in. At first, I am a little taken aback by the process, but after a bit, I find myself glad the army knows I am visiting.

Even though I had not seen military aircraft in the area, the Colombian army's presence was obvious. This was their territory, and they are obviously determined to maintain control.

Once past security, we meet up with the local pastor on the sidewalk in front of the terminal. He arrives on a motorcycle and arranges for a taxi to take us to the hotel. The hotel is about ten minutes from the airport. M.L. had already given me complete details about the day's activities, but the pastor reiterates that all activities will take place at the hotel. We are not to go out wandering around. I am not known for wandering around, but occasionally I take a walk. In all honesty, I would have preferred all of our activities take place *at* the airport. The airport feels more secure. However, I am already aware the army is unwilling to allow it to be used as a meeting place.

As we enter the city of San Jose del Guaviare, it feels as though we have arrived in the Wild West. All roads are dirt roads, except for the main thoroughfare through the center of town. It consists of asphalt covered in dust and dirt. I observe motorcycles as the main mode of transportation, followed by four wheel drive vehicles, then horses. Most of the buildings are only one story, with only a few two-story buildings scattered among them.

A couple of years ago this was FARC country, and even the national government dared not enter the area. The local government was controlled completely by guerrillas and drug lords.

We drive off the main road to the right, down two blocks and then around the corner to the right. As we pull up to the hotel, we encounter a beautiful, new, two-story building. The floors are marble, and everything is freshly painted. It is an extremely nice building.

We register at the desk and move into our rooms in record time. There are already people there waiting to meet with us. We return to the first floor to attend a breakfast meeting with the pastor and his team and are seated at an outdoor table near the pool. If we are meeting for breakfast, *why not here* in such a beautiful place! We spend some time going over the schedule and share what we hope to accomplish that day. The pastor is extremely appreciative that we have come to his city. As we talk about his church and his vision for the city, it is impossible to ignore the excitement in his voice.

My curiosity is stirred over two issues that I want to discuss with the pastor and his team. "Pastor, I am interested in knowing about your problems with the Mafia and the FARC. Did you really have to rip pages from the syllabus so as not to have trouble with these two groups?"

"Oh yes," he replied. "They were going around to homes and churches to see what we were doing. They would flip through the pages of the syllabus, and if they found anything about the United States printed in them, we were accused of being part of the CIA (Central Intelligence Agency) or the DEA (Drug Enforcement Administration). It is too dangerous here. Yes, I did rip pages out, and thank you for changing the format."

I inform the pastor that the diploma has a seal from the United States, but M L. has discussed this with us previously, and we brought a seal from Costa Rica to use instead. I ask him which seal he prefers we use. His response is obvious, "Let's use the one from Costa Rica. It is just too dangerous here, and people's lives are at risk." Before the subject changes, he and his entire group express their thanks for the use of the Bible Institute as a tool to prepare and equip their people.

I comment about the lack of military presence at the airport. He tells me they are on patrol throughout the city. He asks me if the crop dusting planes are still at the airport, and I tell him I had seen them yesterday and again that morning. He tells me they were working with the army. "Oh really? What are they doing?" I ask.

He begins to explain, "Well, it all started about a year ago. The government sent some men in to rip the cocaine plants out by the root and burn them. It was not long before one of the men was killed. The government decided they would not send in any more men, but they would send in planes to fumigate the area instead. They fly over and spray the area where they have reportedly found cocaine to kill off the plants. The only problem is that it kills everything. The truth is, there are many small and large plots of cocaine in the area. Many farmers grow a little on inconspicuous areas of their property. It makes for a nice cash crop. I am not passing judgment. I am simply stating fact. So, when the planes are called in, they spray down the entire area to assure success, but in doing so, they are spraying and thus killing many legitimate crops. The situation gets even more complicated. Imagine. How do you feed your cows if the pasture is dead? I trust the president will come up with another solution. We all know he has accomplished much, but more must be done."

After my conversation with the pastor, I think to myself, San Jose del Guaviare not only looks like the Wild West but living life here sounds pretty wild too! How encouraging to know the Bible Institute can truly touch lives anywhere; even here in San Jose del Guaviare!

The first teaching session begins at 9:00 a.m., and like the day before, I work with the teachers. The curriculum I use for my lessons is called *'Teachers Training.'* Perhaps that is not the most exciting name, but the material is powerful. It is a teaching developed specifically for the Bible Institute because we sought the best way to help our teachers.

We begin by looking at the word *'attitude'* regarding teachers and teaching. What type of attitude should a teacher have? Dictionaries are important tools for a teacher. We utilize a couple of dictionaries to look up the definition for teacher. It is of utmost importance to get a clear understanding of the duties and responsibilities of a teacher. The next step in this hands-on method of teaching is to go to our Bible in the New Testament and look up every place *'teacher'* is mentioned in scripture. We start our research with Jesus and work diligently through the book of Acts. We continue from the book of Acts to the Pauline and General Epistles. In our systematic study, we concur; teaching is a great responsibility, and it is also vital to be of excellent character in order to produce for the Kingdom of God. We conclude our lessons by studying about *'False Teachers'* as mentioned in scripture.

It usually takes a full eight hours to study this material, but today we will only cover half of it in the four hours we have with this group of students, teachers and pastors.

Some of the teachers present have traveled to San Jose del Guaviare while others are residents here. The hotel has set up a nice room for us in the conference center on the second floor. How pleasant it is to be at this fine hotel! Our meeting room is completely open on three sides. While we work, we get to enjoy a gentle blowing breeze and a beautiful view of a section of the city!

What a pleasure to observe these students! You can see their eyes light up as revelation floods their hearts. They pose good questions, and it is pure joy to interact with them in this setting. We answer all of their questions before lunch, and then have hands-on training in regard to student file handling, and other practical applications in the Bible Institute. These training sessions ensure both teachers and students have a positive and enjoyable experience with the Institute.

I was privileged to teach the very first group of students. The Bible Institute began in the small town of Tres Rios, just twenty minutes out of San Jose, Costa Rica. I taught the classes, passed out the weekly homework assignments and even graded the homework. I also distributed quizzes, graded them and kept attendance in a competent manner. Approximately ten weeks

into the classes, feeling I was doing a great job, reality slapped me in the face. In two weeks, the students would be taking their final exam and would be anxious to know their final grade, but I had discovered a major problem. I would not be able to give them their final grade. Why? Because although I knew the proper breakdown for the grading process in regard to attendance, homework and quizzes, I had failed to record those grades anywhere! Humbly, I went to students and asked them for their help. I needed them to return all homework assignments and quizzes so that I could figure their final grade. We soon realized this would be an impossible task. What was I to do; use the grade from the final exam and the attendance percentage to determine the final grade? In the end, I figured it was my mistake not theirs, and everyone scored 100%! However, after that experience, a 'control sheet' was developed. All information pertaining to the student is systematically recorded on a single sheet, which makes recordkeeping quick and easy.

M.L. helps me finish the group activities as I need to get to my room and dress for the graduation ceremony. M.L. prepares the graduates as per protocol. We purchased graduation robes from Bogota for the graduates. A gifted local band came in and set up their equipment. They are to be a part of the graduation. They will not only sing for us but will also lead us in worship. Family and friends are once again in attendance, and one of the graduates has a very special guest; her fiancé from the city of Villavicencio, where we had just had our largest group of graduates. I was just there a few days prior.

Carlos, the fiancé, who was one of our graduates came by motorcycle and shared that it was a dusty ten-hour drive.

We have plenty of time for the graduation ceremony, so I am not the only one that will speak. M.L. shares and encourages the students. The Pastor also shares since all of the students graduating today are from his church. The other churches who participated in the morning sessions still need a few months of study to be ready for graduation; however, the teachers came to support the others and, of course, to see the Bible Institute graduation in San Jose del Guaviare. With only twelve graduates, handing out diplomas goes quickly. We take time to pray for all the graduates and snap a few photos. It is now time for refreshments!

I just sit back and watch the graduates take pictures with their families and look at their diplomas up close. This is truly a big moment for them! For some, it is the first time in their lives they have ever completed their studies and the first time they have received a certificate for their studies!

Tonight is the first night I get to go to bed early, and before I go to bed, I think I will take a *nap!*

Day 9

Goodbye Big B. - Hello Mr. C.

This morning is a beautiful morning! I am convinced the roosters and I are the only ones awake at this hour! As the sun begins to rise, the city begins to stir.

Checkout, today, is problem free. The hotel staff is already helping us move our luggage. Additionally, they are evaluating the damage to the mini-bar in our room. We make our way to the front desk reception area to request a taxi. The taxi arrives, and the process of loading our luggage into the vehicle begins. It requires a bit of maneuvering to load everything in the extremely small vehicle. As we head off to the (SJE) San Jose del Guaviare airport, I am satisfied knowing in less than eleven minutes, we will be back in a secure area.

The taxi driver, like many taxi drivers, is talkative this morning. I just listen as he and M.L. talk about the important happenings in San Jose del Guaviare. I choose not to participate in the conversation; mostly because I do not feel like explaining my accent so early in the morning.

The airport looks the same as we left it yesterday with the Colombian Army providing security. This means we will have to go through security before they allow us in the building. Since there are no X-ray machines or metal detectors, our luggage must be inspected by hand as we are being frisked by army personnel outside on the sidewalk. We must repeat this process once we get inside the airport. We and our luggage will undergo the exact inspection we just completed. The civilian airport security will have their turn next.

We retrieve our boarding passes with no problem, but we did have complications with my luggage. The person at the counter asked me to check my entire luggage so that none would be carried on. I assured him my carry-on would not be a problem since I would hand it to a crew member once I was on board. They would in turn place it in the cargo area inside the aircraft and hand it back to me on the tarmac. A bit perturbed he stated, "Not today. You will check it all here. Now." Well, this was a problem! I had valuable equipment in my carry-on, and I wanted it all to arrive in Bogota. Bottom line? I did not want anything stolen. He assured me he understood my concerns but informed me the luggage would still need to be checked. I then backtracked to a man at a booth who wrapped my luggage in plastic wrap. This would be my best defense to keep anything inside from being taken since there is no way you can get into the bag without making a mess of things.

The plane arrives, and it is truly the smallest aircraft yet. Total capacity is only seventeen passengers; eight on each side with a seat for a third person to sit in the center in the back row. If you have flown, you are familiar with the flight attendant giving instructions before take-off, but on this trip, there is no flight attendant.

The captain enters the plane and closes the door. He slides into his seat, and as he taxis the plane down the runway, he reviews the safety procedures over the intercom. As the aircraft rises, and the wheels lift off the ground, I gaze down at the city of San Jose del Guaviare. I say to myself, "Thank you Lord, for a safe and secure time in both Florencia and here in San Jose." What an honor to serve the one and only living God! The flight was gorgeous, and it wasn't long before we were looking down on the massive city of Bogota.

As soon as I am out of the plane I call home. I have been out of reach the last few days, and I want to make sure everyone and everything is good at home. Marjorie answers the phone. "Yes dear, I am back in Bogota. Everything went well, and for the rest of the trip my phone should have coverage. How is everything back home? Good…Love you!"

A word from
Marjorie Korach

The English language has always been difficult for me; so much so, that in high school I did not study English but French. I never imagined that one day I would marry an American. I met Donald at church. Donald came to Tres Rios to teach weekly classes for a year. It was there that I fell in love with him.

I come from a big family having three brothers and two sisters. Being married to a missionary has not been easy. Donald has to travel frequently, which was something very new for me. The hardest trip for me was when he went to Colombia, and I was six months pregnant. Donald made a seventeen day trip, and it was the first time

I was home alone. A week after Donald returned I had become paralyzed on the right side of my face. My mouth and right eye drooped. For the next month, Donald took me three days a week to rehab. Thankfully, I made a full recovery before Rachel was born.

When Rachel was a baby, she would get sick whenever Donald took a trip. The pediatrician told us she felt the absence of her father. As we prayed for Rachel, she became accustomed to her Dad's traveling. Because it was difficult for the family, Donald decided to limit his trips to two weeks or less. Today, he usually travels less than a week at a time, with a two-week trip only once in a while.

Rachel and Donnie, who are older now, are accustomed to their Father traveling, and I no longer feel alone. Of course, the children keep me very busy. Thanks to phones and computers, it is pretty easy to keep in contact with Donald.

Marjorie Korach

As I finish my call with Marjorie, I am thankful to the Lord I was able to be home for important dates in my children's lives; such as their graduations.

I woke up in Cali and took a taxi to the airport. Even though I had a group of thirty-five people in the country, I left them and headed home. I left a very qualified young man in charge. He was to take care of them on their 'touristy day' and

then get them to the airport the following day. I could not stay as I had a very important appointment in San Jose, Costa Rica. If the flight from Cali to Panama and the one from Panama to Costa Rica were all on schedule, I would make it back home with two hours to spare.

The first flight left on time, and the second was on time as well. I am going to make it! Now all I needed was a fast taxi driver to get me home. Rachel was graduating from Preparatory that day; something I simply could not miss. I walked into the house, changed my clothes and drove to the school. As I sat in the graduation ceremony of little Rachel, I didn't think about the group that was still in Cali or the ministry we had just accomplished in Colombia. I was overwhelmed with gratitude that I made it there on time. I sat in the third row and took pictures as tears flooded my eyes. All I could do was say, "Thank you Jesus! Thank you, for making sure I was here for this."

Another important day was Donnie's graduation from Preparatory. I was in Tegucigalpa, Honduras. Once again, I was with a group, and once again, I was going to leave them, at least for a little while. There was an early flight straight from Tegucigalpa to San Jose that morning, and there was another one back there late that afternoon. I made it back to the house with about two hours to spare. "Donnie, are you ready for the graduation?" Oh, yes, he was ready...and "Do you have your bags packed?" He assured me that his bags were packed, and he was ready to go! You see, after the graduation, Donnie and I would be going directly from the school to the airport. We would go to Tegucigalpa to complete the last two days of ministry, and then I would drive the van back home.

The graduation was nice, and I was once again very grateful that I could be there for such an important occasion. Donnie made one last attempt to bring his mother with us since it would be the first time he has gone without her, but this was to be a special 'father and son' trip. So, once we were past the 'Mother' hurdle, we hopped into a waiting taxi, and we were off to the airport to catch our plane.

We checked in but had to take some additional steps to get through immigration since Donnie was a minor. The head of immigration came out and talked to us a few minutes to make sure everything was legitimate. The head of immigration that day was an old neighbor of mine; so of course, we had no problems with clearance.

Donnie was excited about the flight. He had been on planes before, and he knew what to expect. Since this was the last flight out to Honduras for the day, it meant we would not be traveling on a large plane but in a smaller prop plane. Donny was not happy with this arrangement, but we made the flight and had a great time in Honduras and on the return trip as well. Traveling by land was an adventure of sorts for both Donnie and myself.

All of our luggage arrives with us. This is a very good thing. We are only going to be at (BOG) Bogota long enough to catch another flight to (CLO) Cali. It is time to make our way back to the counter area in the airport and find our next carrier for the day. They will not allow me any carry-on luggage either. However, I am allowed to carry on a couple of things: my Bible, teaching notes, and the certificates for the graduates. Having these items on hand means the graduation ceremony will happen on time, luggage, or no luggage.

As we walk to the gate, we have just enough time to find a cup of coffee and a donut. I know just the place, and it is conveniently located on the way to security. This time, we walk to a gate where the big planes are kept. As we board, M.L. seems a bit more relaxed. She does not enjoy the little planes.

I enjoy the cool air of Bogota. On this trip, it is the last time I will feel the refreshing air in this high city. The rest of the trip will be warm, even hot in comparison since our next stop was Cali.

The flight to Cali was just under an hour. The (CLO) Cali airport, like in most places is not in the city. In fact, it is in a totally different town. This town is surrounded by sugar cane fields, which makes it an interesting place since one can see sugar cane fields in all directions and as far as the eye can see.

Our arrival is quick and easy. I appreciate the design of the (CLO) Cali airport. I have always liked it because of its unique layout. It not only allows you to see the planes coming in and out, but you also hear them as they roll up to the gate or roar down the runway during takeoff.

Within fifteen minutes, we have our luggage in hand, and we are walking out the door. The person sent to retrieve us is waiting. In only a few moments, we are driving down the road on our way to Cali. I have made this trip many times, and I know we are about an hour from our destination. Our driver is a nice man from one of the churches. He will be with us for the next two days and assures me he is up for the task.

It's great to be back in Santiago de Cali, more simply known as Cali. It was the first big city to embrace the Bible Institute. When I visited there the first time, I observed a growing and prosperous city. I soon learned that a major drug cartel had a great deal of influence over this city. Thankfully, things have changed for the better since then. The Government of Colombia put the squeeze on the cartel, and they chased them all around the city and region until they were all captured or killed.

On one of my visits to the city during those days, the atmosphere in the city was tense and fear-filled. The skies were full of government helicopters seeking and eliminating known drug dealers. It was only a few weeks after that trip that the grip of the cartel was broken, and the people began to relax. However, the victory over the drug dealers was a double-edged sword. The upside was that the people and the Gospel had more freedom than ever before. The flipside was not so positive, as the people of Cali quickly learned that their prosperous economy was a façade. With the ousting of the cartel, the money dried up, and it took over five years for Cali's economy to regain its footing.

On my last trip to Cali, I took a taxi to the mall instead of going directly to my hotel to call Marjorie and the kids. On the way to the mall, I noticed some of the streets were closed. A car bomb had just exploded in the area. The taxi began to make his detour around the problem area, but as he did, another bomb exploded a block or so ahead of us. We got away from that location as quickly as we could. We decided to drive to the other side of the city for me to make my call home. I suppose I should have simply headed back to the hotel and attempted to make my call the next day.

Obviously, Cali has had its share of problems, but in spite of those problems or maybe because of them, Cali has been *a place where the people have been very open to the Gospel. Since our early days in this city, the Bible Institute has blossomed, and we have had the privilege of holding many graduations there. It was in Cali that we had our first graduation ceremony of five hundred students!*

We check into the hotel. It will be our center of operation as teachers would be arriving in less than an hour, and the graduates will arrive this evening. I have been at this hotel many times, and the staff knows me well, as they are the ones who worked with me to pull the mini-bar early when a large group was here with me.

There is an assembly of pastors waiting to have lunch with us. All of the travel has made us a little late, but we have tried our best to stay on schedule. All is well, and once we are situated and freshened up, it is time to meet with the pastors. They are pastors who represent an indigenous group of people. I did not catch whether they called themselves a tribe or nation. No matter, they came to talk with me about how we could get the Bible Institute on their reservation to help their pastors and churches. It is an interesting lunch to say the least.

M.L. works on all the details of the graduation ceremony while I spend time with the teachers. We review session one and then session two with a refreshment break between the two reviews. We have a great time together as we study and share the Word of God.

Some of the teachers will be graduating later in the day, but all will be staying to support their graduating students. After I finish the sessions, M.L. hands me a stack of diplomas needing my signature and assures me this is all that is pending for the graduation ceremony. I ask her to leave them here as I will return in a few minutes. I hurry up to my room and get ready for the graduation ceremony. While the graduates and family members arrive, I find a table where I can complete the graduation certificates for Cali with my signature. The hotel's conference room is too small, and once again the crowd gathers in the hallway and around the outside of the room.

We have no music, not even a guitar player, but this is a good thing since the room is packed with people. I'm not sure where we would have placed musicians. We did, however, have a singer. He is very good as he leads us a cappella in a wonderful time of praise and worship. I was hoping we would simply sing all night, but eventually it is time for me to minister to the graduates. There are six churches represented, and everyone is gathered to celebrate the one hundred and nine graduating students from the city of Cali.

I realize handing out this many diplomas will take a while. It is a delight to watch as each church applauds their classmates and friends from other churches. We see all kinds of things in a graduation ceremony like this one. We see those who cry because they are so excited about their accomplishment, and then we may see a young man who looks like he is ready to jump out of his skin! One of the most special sites is seeing an entire family of both parents and young adults graduating in the same service. It is a fantastic and gratifying time for everyone involved!

After the photos and hugs, it is time to think about tomorrow and its unique schedule. The Bible Institute has had the privilege of celebrating many graduations, but tomorrow's agenda will bring some extra challenges. I need to make sure everything (each moving part) is in order before I lay my head to rest for the night.

My thoughts are interrupted when M.L. drops by to give me an update from the driver. He had called to inform us tomorrow is a *'no car day'* in Cali. This means that by 5:30 a.m. all streets will be completely closed to vehicle traffic. You might say it is Cali's way of going green and helping save the planet. I end my conversation with, "Ok, no car day in Cali. So, what time do we need to leave the hotel to be past the no drive zone by 5:30 a.m.? See you then, Good night!" I go straight to my room knowing that morning will come too quickly.

Day 10

Three Graduations and One Embarrassed Dean!

"Good morning everyone!" I greet M.L and the driver cheerfully on a day that started very early for all of us. I find I am wondering if we will make it out of the city in time. We do not want to be locked in when the streets are closed off. Our driver assures me we will make it in time but suggests we leave as soon as possible-just to be sure. It looks like the entire city is under construction. There is major construction happening to the main thoroughfare and of course, like most government projects, they were way over budget and way behind schedule. Cali is building their version of transmilenio and calling it *El Mio*. Hopefully, within six to twelve months, Cali will be restored, and its citizens recovered from all that has transpired in recent years.

Today, we will be doing something we have not done thus far as a ministry. We are going to have three graduations in three different cities all on the same day. Our first ceremony is scheduled to begin at 10:00 a.m. in Pradera.

Pradera is part of the department of Valle de Cauca. Cali is the capital of the Valle de Cauca. Pradera is a pleasant town just on the other side of the airport where my plane landed yesterday; the one surrounded by sugar cane. In fact, in October they celebrate the *'Day of Candy.'* This is likely due to sugar cane being the main source of the area's economy. There are many huge Igenios (factories) where the cane is processed into sugar.

Driving past the Cali airport floods my mind with memories of what the Lord has done for me while on this road.

Years ago, I was traveling this exact road in a bus with a group ready to minister, but my heart and focus was on my daughter back in Costa Rica. About a month before the trip, we were sitting at our kitchen table with a neighbor. Rachel began to complain about having muscle cramps (like a charley-horse) in her legs. Neither Marjorie nor I thought much of it. As soon as Rachel left the table, our neighbor who was a physical therapist at the hospital informed us it was not normal for children to have muscle cramps. It is normal for adults but not for children. She recommended we pay close attention to the situation. The muscle cramps continued for a few days, and we took Rachel to see her pediatrician. He gave us some medicine and told us if she didn't improve in a day or two, take her to see a specialist.

Days passed with no improvement. At this point, Rachel not only had muscle cramps but she could not walk. I discovered she was crawling around the house because walking was too painful.

The specialist also prescribed medication, but he wanted to run more tests before coming to any conclusions. At the end of the tests, which included running electric shock through Rachel's legs, he diagnosed a classic case of Guillain-Barr Syndrome.

As I understand it, Guillain-Barr Syndrome is a viral disease that affects the nervous system. In Guillain-Barr Syndrome, the body's defense system attacks the virus, but the virus is cloaked so that it looks like a part of the nervous system. The body's natural defense system gets confused and destroys the nervous system by mistake. It starts in the feet and moves up the legs. If not stopped, it will make its way up into the respiratory system eventually causing death. The sensation in your legs becomes extremely painful, and you stop walking. You go from being a normal, healthy individual, to sitting in a wheelchair and eventually become bedridden.

Marjorie would take Rachel in for the final tests as I was leaving for Colombia. What an emotional conversation Marjorie and I had as she broke the news via telephone. The Doctor's suspicions were confirmed. Guillain-Barr Syndrome was the diagnosis. Of course, Marjorie and I had been praying about the situation, but that seemed little comfort at that moment because we were miles apart. This only made this trying time more difficult.

Our local pastor David Salazar was aware of the situation. They planned to go over to the house and pray for Rachel the following day. She was missing classes at school as moving around had become quite complicated. The pastor arrived with his wife the following evening and prayed for Rachel, anointing her with oil. The next morning Rachel woke up pain-free and went to school. She was scheduled for additional testing, and I was aware the tests were painful for her. This time, however, the doctor came back with a very different report. He said he could tell from the tests that some nerves had been damaged, but now they were healed. There was evidence the disease had existed and signs of the resulting damage to the nerves, but it had ceased to exist. It seemed her immune system had figured out the difference between nerve and virus!

Marjorie called me back with this wonderful report, and the dark clouds immediately lifted! I was traveling on this road when I declared the goodness of God and shared this powerful testimony with the group!

Would it surprise you to know the devil tested us on this one more time? Exactly one year later the symptoms returned and once again, I was heading to Colombia. Needless to say, Marjorie and I were distraught. We returned to the specialist to find out what was happening. We wondered if it was something new or if it was related to the initial problem. He had told us that once the immune system had figured out how to attack the virus that we were out of the woods. He informed us now that in ninety-nine percent of these cases there are no repeat incidents. However, though a rare occurrence, the Guillain-Barr Syndrome can mutate and go on the attack again.

As a parent, what do you do? I can tell you what we did; we prayed! With this news, they immediately ran the tests again. Initially, Rachel had not known what to expect, but this time she knew it would be painful, and that made things more difficult. It is a joy to report that approximately two weeks after this happened, all symptoms, and all pain disappeared and never returned. From time to time, like any normal child, Rachel comes home from school and says those scary words to us, "My leg hurts." When this happens, time stops for a moment for Marjorie and me. However, after a quick review of her daily activities, we find she has had a sporting event or a PE class or something quite normal that is likely the cause of her discomfort. We watch her closely for the next few days, just to be sure, but we rest in God knowing He hears and answers our prayers!

We pull into town just as businesses are opening their doors. We find a quaint little place whose specialty is serving fresh Colombian pastries and delicious Colombian coffee. It is interesting to watch people as they are on their way to work. It doesn't take long before a young man selling the daily newspaper spots us enjoying a little breakfast. We soon become his next customer as we enjoy our breakfast at the sidewalk café.

Shortly after breakfast, we contact the pastor who is hosting this morning's graduation. Initially, he seems a bit concerned that we have arrived so early, but it is not a problem. We meet him at the church, and this gives us an opportunity to fellowship before the graduates arrive. Before long, people join us. It seems like everyone arrives at the same time, but perhaps that is because they all rode on the same bus. The musicians are here to help, which surprises me. I did not expect a full service so early in the morning. We proceed with the graduation protocol; things go smoothly and quickly. There are only twenty-four graduates, so it does not take long.

I go upstairs to one of the classrooms to change clothes and get ready for the graduation. I have prepared both my travel clothes and graduation clothes for the day, but suddenly I have an idea. Since the graduation robe is long, I figure no will notice that I am wearing my blue jeans this morning. After dressing, I take two steps into the main sanctuary and M.L. intercepts me and says, "Don, you can't wear jeans to a graduation! You are the Dean of the Bible Institute." So much for my good idea! I am back upstairs one last time to change into correct graduation clothing.

We have a wonderful time with the first group of graduates from Pradera. The Pastor has prepared a very special toast for the occasion, but as soon as he finished the toast, and we have eaten a piece of cake to share in the celebration, it is time to run! We must make it to graduation number two!

Our drive to the next location is supposed to take two hours. About an hour into the drive I am awakened by rain pelting the windshield. In the tropics, you can have light rainfall, or it can pour! There is a term we use in Spanish for when it rains hard. The term is *'aguacero.'* It sounds like *zero* or *no water*, but it actually means *lots of rain*. This term caught my interest, so I asked my friends and my Costa Rican family, "When it rains a lot, why do you say aguacero?" Oddly enough; no one knew. They would say, "You're right. It sounds strange, but that is just the way it is!" After some searching, I finally found the word's origin. It is a term used by meteorologists meaning the water is causing zero visibility. *Aguacero* now makes sense to me, and I can assure you we experienced *aguacero* that day!

The driver pulls off the road a few times because he is unable to see a thing! It is simply too dangerous not to stop. It rains like this for an hour, but then suddenly it is gone! We continue to drive through an area where you might never know it was raining so hard only minutes before. The rain delays our arrival at the site for graduation number two-the city of Cartago. This rain delay reminds me of another day of risky driving.

My parents came down for a visit when I was still single. I had planned their schedule, and this time we were going to make a trip to San Carlos and then travel on to see the Monteverde Rainforest. Both are very nice places, but perhaps we should not have planned both on the same trip.

The road to San Carlos from San Jose is a dangerous road to travel. There are many tight curves as the road wraps around the mountains. Additionally, you must share the road with lots of big trucks and thick traffic going in both directions. It is a beautiful trip if one travels on a clear day, but if you drive at night, or in the fog, it can prove to be fatal.

That day I took my parents around the mountain to get to San Carlos. I don't drive slowly, nor do I speed. I just go. My friend Nago is from San Carlos, so we stopped to see him before continuing our trip. We hopped into the car to get breakfast, but when I stepped on the brakes, I found out that there were no brakes! My Dad was upset, but it only took him a second to remember where we were just a few minutes before. We were zipping around the mountains on our way and might have lost our lives had the brakes gone out on the winding, mountainous road. It was a little difficult to get upset knowing how we had been spared from what could have been a tragedy.

We found a mechanic, and though it took all morning to get the car fixed, we left San Carlos with safe brakes. Our destination? A hotel on the other side of the Arenal Volcano. I had to leave my car in the town of Fortuna, and we had to take a 4x4 taxi the rest of the way to get to the hotel. We had to forge a couple rivers on the way. This turned our trip into quite an adventure. Of course, by the time we arrived it was already dark and had clouded over. Not very impressive. However, in the middle of the night, the volcano began to let off some steam and things started shaking. We never saw the volcano, but you sure could feel it! I wondered if this is how the people of Israel felt when Moses went up to Mount Sinai.

This visit was difficult for my parents thus far. We had the scare due to the brake failure, and then we experienced the rumbling and shaking of the volcano all through the night. It seems that would be more than enough--but the best was yet to come!

I decided to take them to Montverde Reserve. People come from around the world to go through this huge private reserve. I had two options to get us there. We could go back up the mountain road we had driven down by the grace of God yesterday and go out to the main road. We would then need to travel several more hours as this was a four to five-hour trip. Another option was to go around Lake Arenal, out to Guanacaste, get on the main road and do the same thing as the first option only from the other direction. Again, a four or five-hour drive. Then I heard about option three; the short cut! Well, you guessed it; I opted for the shortcut!

We began traveling. It didn't take long before the asphalt road became a dirt road, and then the dirt road turned into a trail. We were literally on the top of the mountain looking down on farmland. We eventually arrived, but during our journey we saw country we had never seen before or since! Just for the record, the short cut took four and a half hours!

A word from
Don and Sandy Korach Sr.

The scenery was beautiful, but the roads were the worst I have ever experienced. Holes as big as the car, we were in the middle of nowhere with no food, no water and no sign of life for hours. After about two hours into the trip, we came upon a small horse-drawn funeral procession. A man's death was the first sign of life in hours. About an hour further into the trip I was surprised to see a truck hauling a sheet of plate glass on a gravel road, not the cow path we had been traveling on earlier. From that point on, I had hopes that civilization, food and water were not far away!

It is always an adventure traveling with my son. He always says that half the fun is getting there!

**Don and Sandy Korach Sr.
Minnesota**

Upon arrival at the church, we saw that people were all ready for the service. The graduates are ready and dressed in their robes. The guests are seated, and the music is playing. Even though everyone is ready, I still need to get ready, and we must complete the graduation protocol. Everybody waits patiently while some of the students help us prepare for the service. We are using the home church building where some of the graduates attend. Four different churches are represented in this graduating class. The site was chosen because it is a central location for those coming in from cities on the north, south and east.

Included in this group of graduates are some friends from Armenia, the first Colombian city to embrace the Bible Institute. It is always special to reflect on what was initiated several years ago and see how it continues to produce for the Kingdom of God. It is great to see old friends, and though we are here to celebrate the graduates, we find time to catch up as we talk about families and ministries.

Armenia is the capital city of Quindío. It will always be a special department to the Bible Institute and me. It was the first place that embraced the vision for the Institute. When the Bible Institute was introduced to Colombia, the churches in the area clamored to have the teachings in their churches. They immediately recognized the potential of this powerful tool and the impact it could have on their people. They embraced it with enthusiasm and could not wait to begin!

The department of Quindío is coffee country. It produces some of the best coffee in Colombia, if not the best in the world. It grows on beautiful rolling hills. In fact, there is an amusement park in Armenia called 'Coffee Park.' At the park, you are greeted by huge signs of the famous Juan Valdez.

Growing coffee takes great knowledge and skill. It cannot be in a climate that is too hot or too cold. The plants enjoy mountains with just enough sunshine and rainfall. Armenia is a picturesque place with great weather. It has become a tourist magnet with many people acquiring summer or weekend homes in the region. The department of Quindio is the smallest of all the departments in Colombia and is hidden in the foothills of the Andes Mountains. It was here that the Lord brought us so that we might begin reaching the people of Colombia. The thought of that reminds me of **Zechariah 4:10, "For who hath despised the day of small things?"** *Just as Zerubbabel's task may have seemed small and insignificant to some, no work accomplished with the blessing of God is trivial. Every building begins with breaking ground by scooping one* *shovel of dirt on an empty lot.* **Zechariah 4:6 says, "This is the word of the Lord...Not by might, nor by power, but by My Spirit saith the Lord of hosts."** *From this small place, Quindío, Colombia, God launched the Bible Institute, which would continue to stretch out to the entire nation.*

Over time, I have learned a lesson traveling to and from Armenia and Quindío. Once you've completed the agenda on any given trip, it is easy to relax, kick back and begin to think about going home. I have since learned to set aside the 'kick back mode' and enter what I call the 'not one step back mode.' Why? Armenia has a tiny airport. More than once I have been told a flight was late or canceled. Sometimes I've been offered a nonchalant "We'll see you tomorrow." When I enter 'not one step back' mode, I am going forward no matter what! If that means I must wait for the next flight out, I will. Nevertheless, I am not going back to the city. I am staying put until they fly me out in the direction of home. Of course, I realize there are legitimate delays, but I do not drop my guard for even a second, as I have one goal in mind--getting back home!

Just before it is my turn to share God's Word with graduates, they begin singing a song one of the pastors had written. The words of this song bring encouragement to my heart. They express how their lives have been changed and impacted by the ministry of the Word of God through the Bible Institute. The commitment, prayer, and sacrifices involved in making all of this possible have proven to be fruitful, and all of the glory goes to the Lord!

After ministering the Word, handing out diplomas and taking a few pictures, it is time for the students to toss their caps into the air with a shout. "One, two, three!" and with a hallelujah the forty-eight caps go flying up in the air. However, only forty-seven came back down. One of the caps pokes a hole in the ceiling and stays! I laugh so hard! Perhaps I should be embarrassed, but it is quite funny!

With the ceremony complete, I am pleased to find that our friends here in Cartago have shown great hospitality in preparing a delicious meal for us.

An 'arepa' is one of the typical foods in Colombia. Not all arepas are the same. Each region or city prepares them in their own unique way. I was introduced to arepas in Armenia and thoroughly enjoyed them. However, when I went to another city, the arepas were completely different, and honestly, I was not very impressed. When in Armenia, I always found someone selling arepas, which was not difficult since there was one on every corner. I made sure to wear a shirt with short sleeves when purchasing arepas because it is imperative if you want to enjoy eating them. You see; as you stand on the corner and enjoy every bit of your warm, flat, cooked corn flour dough, the butter of that Armenian arepa will drip right down to your elbows! Wow! They are out of this world!

When the students from Armenia graduated, they went all out by making me fresh, homemade Armenian arepas. Their beautiful gesture made our time there extra special. Though, I must confess; I ate them from a plate using a fork and knife on this occasion. After all, the Dean could not be seen with a buttery elbows!

As soon as we finish eating, we say our farewells and begin making our way to the third and final graduation of the day. Our next stop is Pereira, a small modern city right in the middle of coffee country. I sit back to enjoy the ride, allowing my thoughts to take me back to my home, family, and especially to my daughter Rachel.

When Rachel was only three months old, Marjorie and I took her to the national registry to apply for her passport. Costa Rica is very protective of children. Acquiring a child's passport requires an extensive legal process, which in a word can be described as frustrating. When filling out the paperwork, there was a question regarding Rachel's eye color. As you may know, it sometimes takes a while for children's eyes to settle on a color. Both Marjorie and I have brown eyes, but we had hoped Rachel would have her grandmother's blue eyes. At the time, we confidently filled out the papers indicating her eyes were hazel. In fact, they were at that time, but within a few weeks, Rachel's eyes changed to brown. For the next five years, Rachel's passport indicated that her eyes were hazel.

With passport process complete, at three months of age, Rachel took her first missions trip to Armenia, Colombia with her mother in tow. She did a fabulous job! Everyone fussed over her and took turns carrying her around. She was a charming, beautiful baby!

The trip over to Pereira is fairly quick. Our driver stops for directions to the hotel. It seems like a nice place and will serve as operation central for the rest of the day's events. It is time to say goodbye to our driver, but I want to make sure he receives a good tip in addition to the amount previously agreed on for his services. He has done a fabulous job, and we surely could not have made it to all of the graduation ceremonies on time without him.

We check in at the hotel, but by the time I get to my room, it is already time to go back down to the conference center where the graduation ceremony will be held. I ask M.L. to take care of everything, and I promise to get there before the singing ends. I am beginning to feel a bit tired and need a few minutes to get ready.

The walk over to the conference room is fascinating! I leave the main building, walk around pools and lighted, winding paths to reach the conference center building. As I walk in, I am greeted by the pastor who advises me they are ready to begin the service. All of the graduates are dressed in their graduation robes, and they are all wearing huge smiles along with their caps. Everyone looks beautiful as family and friends have also dressed up for the occasion. There is a special addition to this evening's service; we will have the help of a pastor from another church in the city who will be the M.C. for graduation this evening! This makes the ceremony extra special!

I feel blessed as I sit and listen to a few testimonies from students regarding their time and experience with the Bible Institute. We will honor forty-two graduates; all from the same church. Their Pastor shares a few words before my introduction and address to the graduates. I again joked about them having to take one last test, but I do not take the blame for assigning the test. This time, I blame the pastor and make our National Director M.L. the hero. Everyone roars with emotion and joy!

I comment on how nice everyone looks in their graduation robes before sharing the Word of God. I then jump in with both feet, and find I am up to my neck in one slip of the tongue! In Spanish, we call graduation robes *togas*, but with a slight slip of the tongue, I have taken all the graduates out of their graduation robes and placed them in string bikini bathing suits by saying *tangas* instead! Thank God everyone laughs! The pastor falls out of his seat and onto the floor because he is laughing so hard! *So, what do I do now?* What *can* I do? The more I talk, the worse it will get, so I just laugh along with everyone else. Eventually, I find my way to my Bible, and we all focus on the message. The toga/tanga blooper will surely go down as a vivid memory for this group, but more importantly, everyone is having a great time at their graduation!

I will meet with the teachers and pastors in the morning, and we will once again look at what the Bible says about teachers. I want to meet privately with the pastor, but I think I will get some sleep first. I can't afford to make any additional language bloopers!

Day 11

The Andes Mountains Make Colombia

It sure is nice to be in Pereira!

Pereira is a modern, industrial city on the edge of coffee country. It is the capital of the Department of Risaralda, an important urban center, due to its strategic location in the coffee producing area of Colombia. The three largest cities of Colombia are Bogota, Cali, and Medellin. If you look at a map, you will notice that connecting them with a straight line from one city to the next almost forms a triangle. Who is in the middle of that triangle? Pereira! Being surrounded by all three major cities places Pereira in an excellent location.

Pereira has excellent weather and a comfortable climate, but the unique draw to Pereira is its people. Since the first Spanish settlers arrived, the people and their descendants have continued to make this a wonderful place to live. The people from Antioquia, an area around the city of Medellin, are the ones who have had the most influence in the area. They are people famous for their ingenuity. They are resourceful and hardworking business people. We have heard it said *'the business of business is business.'* In Colombia, if there is any business in the making, a person from Antioquia is taking part, or there is no real business happening.

There is a Spanish saying that I have even heard in Costa Rica and other Central American countries. The saying is, *'hicieron su Agosto'* or directly translated, *'they made their August.'* This means that someone made a good deal or received a good profit. I always find it interesting to discover the origin of cultural sayings. Pereira is a city with many festivals, and the saying *'hicieron su Agosto'* has its origin in Pereira. One of the festivals of the city is in August, so if they sell a great deal of merchandise at the festival, they have made their August.

Pereira has a twin city just like the twin cities of Minneapolis and Saint Paul, Minnesota. The twin city of Pereira is Dosquebradas. Within the metropolitan area that includes these twin cities and three other towns, there are close to one million residents. This is one of the most densely populated areas in Colombia, yet it is special because it continues to hold that small town feeling.

I am getting ready to walk downstairs and attend a meeting with some key pastors from Pereira when my phone rings. It is a call from the office in Costa Rica. "Hello, Elmer! How are you doing?"

A word from
Pastor Elmer Flores:

A short time ago, Dr. Korach and I were sharing at a leadership conference in Colombia. I was scheduled to share at the conference later in the day, so I was reviewing my notes and meditating on the subject I would be teaching. I began thinking about people God had placed in my life as mentors; those who worked to prepare me for the work of the ministry. These people were instrumental in teaching, training and forming me to work in a leadership role for Kingdom of God. The name Donald Korach was the first name to come to me. His name is at the top of my short list.

One of the sessions I would be teaching at this conference was called 'The Law of Legacy.' This law talks about the need to train others so as to leave a legacy here on earth before going home (to heaven). This was when the name Donald Korach resurfaced.

I have had contact with Donald Korach since 1998. As a student of the Bible Institute, Donald was one of my teachers from 1998 to 2002. After I had graduated from the Institute in 2002, I worked on various projects with Donald. I have been a member of the Mutual Faith, Costa Rica team since 2003.

I Thank God for the ministry of Donald Korach. I have been transformed in many areas; in my thinking, in the way I see things and in how I operate in ministry. In working with this ministry, I have learned the value of hearing the words "Well done!" once a project is complete. I have learned the importance of sowing the Word of God into others and the value of taking the gospel to countries and places where violence may scare away other ministers.

I have also learned that God has plans for us that reach far beyond what we can understand or see.

My life has been greatly changed. I have gone from a child in the ministry to a mature member of the Body of Christ. I have gone from having a desire to help to truly working and serving. I have gone from being shut up in my own little Christian world, to affecting and impacting the lives of people around me. I see the need to pass the baton to others, as I understand that the generation that will follow me needs to be trained and I cannot reach everyone. I inherited these values from someone who left his home in Minnesota thirty years ago to impact the world without knowing what was before him.

Today, not only has my life been changed, but thousands of people in Latin America. Conferences, seminars, teachings, and the Bible Institute have all been touched by the ministry of Donald Korach.

As I write these words, I am reminded of a trip we took to Nicaragua. I met with a pastor who has a church of nearly a thousand people. The Pastor commented on the powerful influence a conference he attended in San Jose, Costa Rica had on him. Donald Korach had organized the Mutual Faith International Conference. The pastor's exact words were, "When I plan an event in the church, I compare it to the conference in San Jose so that it has the same quality of teaching and is as well organized."

With Dr. Korach, I have had the opportunity to travel and take the Word of God throughout Central America and parts of South America. There is always a sacrifice involved as one has to pay a price to travel to churches, meet with pastors and provide them training. It is good to see inside Donald's heart and know his desire to train and disciple others. I remember occasions where we have traveled to various Central America nations. It can get complicated crossing borders, and at times we must hurry to get across the border before they close. Sometimes it is hard to find a place to stay. I remember nights we were exhausted but traveled to get to a country to hold a conference for two hundred pastors. On a different occasion, we traveled for a conference of seven thousand! I mention this only because perhaps some people might think that with all the inconveniences in traveling, dealing with other cultures, dealing with different people, pastors, languages, borders, etc., it would be easier just to change one's focus to something 'closer to home.' However, none of these things has ever stopped Donald Korach. As time passes, he continues to focus on the vision of making disciples, and I see him continuing to plan to reach nations with the gospel.

I write these words while in Guatemala. This day marks two weeks of travel in four different countries for us. We have held an International Conference in two countries, celebrated graduations, and held meetings with Pastors and teachers. I still have five days before returning home to rest. We will then return to the office to plan our next activity in order to teach/train others for God's work in the Kingdom. It is so exciting! God bless you!

In Christ,

Pastor Elmer Flores,
Director of IITB
Mutual Faith, Costa Rica

I finish my conversation with Elmer and walk to my breakfast meeting. I begin to chuckle to myself as I remember some of the trips Elmer and I have made together. You know; crossing borders is always interesting. If you are in Costa Rica and travel to Nicaragua, it generates a distinctive level of stress. The more I think about it, the more I am glad in to be in Colombia today.

Borders are necessary. If you do not have borders, you cannot have a country. As much as I have traveled in and out of these countries over the years, I still sometimes wonder if they will let me in or back out of some of the places I've ministered in.

We were traveling from Costa Rica to Honduras. Our International Conference was being held in Tegucigalpa, the capital of Honduras. This was our first international conference out of Costa Rica, so it was very exciting!

The car was loaded down. There were three friends of mine, who were pastors in Costa Rica that wanted to attend the conference, so they accompanied Elmer Flores and myself. The plan was simple; make the trip to Honduras by land. It is sometimes the execution of said plan that can prove to be complex. You see, Costa Rica does not border Honduras. We must leave Costa Rica, enter Nicaragua, cross Nicaragua and then enter Honduras. The total drive time for this trip was approximately sixteen hours. The tricky part, however, was crossing the borders before they closed, preventing us from passing through. So, we carefully planned our trip. We knew that in order to get across Nicaragua's border and then several hours later into Honduras before it closed, we must be at the

Nicaraguan border when it opened in the morning. San Jose is roughly five hours from the northern border. It would mean an extremely early start for our day.

As planned, we arrived at the border and were out of Costa Rica within twenty minutes. Now, we had to cross into Nicaragua. Everything seemed as though it would only take only a few minutes. Then the customs person approached me and asked for the owner of my SUV. Informing me there was a problem, he continued, "I need you and your vehicle to follow me to our storage building."

The rest of the team stayed in the main building when Mr. Follow Me, got into my vehicle and told me where to drive. He took me way back to an old building filled with vehicles. I played the waiting game as he left to assemble a crew of guys who were supposed to take my SUV apart. After an hour of waiting, Mr. Follow Me said, "Ok, you can go." He didn't have to tell me twice!

As I pulled up to the main building, the rest of the guys looked as though they had just returned from a major prayer meeting. They were not happy since they had no idea what had been going on with me. They began to ask, "What happened? What did they want? Did they ask you for money?"

My response was "Guys, just get in the car; it's time to leave!"

The 'excuse' given for their need to take apart and search the vehicle was that they had received a report stating a blue SUV was coming through the border filled with drugs. Therefore, they were required to detain every blue SUV. None of us really believed that story. It was more likely they were looking to acquire some money, but if they were looking for a bribe, they had come to the wrong guy. I have never played that game, and I did not plan to start then. In the end, it was only an inconvenience, as well as great opportunity to pray!

On another occasion, something else odd happened. It was the first day of the month, and as we crossed the Nicaraguan border, we were faced with much confusion and a parking lot full of desks! We found a place to park and walked up to the main building, paperwork in hand. We had to get things in order for both us and our vehicle to enter the country.

The guard informed us that beginning that day, no one was allowed inside the building; this included employees. We were told to go to a desk in another area to receive help. Well, for the next few minutes we went from desk to desk and stood in line after line for all of the proper signatures and seals. It was obvious something had gone wrong, and all of the employees were in trouble. Some executive, in an office located miles from the border, made a decision that was hindering employees and frustrating the visitors entering the country. My heart went out to these guys. I would only be there for a short time. Then I would be back in my air-conditioned vehicle, but they would be there all day in their new, open-air, extremely hot office!

Okay, I admit that I have been in Nicaragua many times. You see, starting the Bible Institute in a new location requires many trips, but the day of the dogs and the screwdrivers in Nicaragua is something I just have to share. That, along with our return trip and the absent police officer, who was found at the local…Well, I'll just let you read it for yourself.

We arrived at the Nicaraguan border with no delays. We were anxious to get through the process as quickly as possible and continue on our way. First, there was Passport Control, where they took our passports. After a few minutes of paperwork, they stamped it showing we were now officially in the country. Next, it was our turn at the police department. They would look the car over and make sure all the numbers corresponded to the paperwork. As we walked out of the office building, the police officer asked us which one was our vehicle. As I pointed out the vehicle, he told us that another man would take care of us. The young man was waiting for us by the car.

I had just purchased the van a few months earlier, and this was its first trip out of the country. I was looking forward to the trip because the van is so comfortable to drive. The young man told us to open the vehicle and to take out the luggage. We placed the luggage to one side. Then, another couple of men arrived, armed with screwdrivers and a dog. Before I knew what was happening, the dog jumped into the van through the back door and made his way through my car. I wasn't happy about this but thought, "Well, it's okay. We're almost finished here," but then the men armed with screwdrivers began taking my car apart! They wanted to look under the flooring and inside the doors. My biggest concern was whether or not they would put it back together again. My first thought had been that I would have to get my car cleaned to get rid of the dog hair, but now I was having visions of a trip to a mechanic to repair all that the screwdriver brigade had destroyed!

When they asked me how to take the dashboard apart, I lost it! I responded, "Listen guy! You guys are the ones with the screwdrivers! I have no idea! And besides, I like it just the way it is!"

Eventually, they said we could go. Before loading our bags back into the vehicle, I asked if they wanted to look inside of our bags and he said, "No, not today." Wow! They wanted to look inside my dashboard but not inside my luggage!

On our return trip, they had another surprise waiting. Once again, passport control was no problem, and in just a few minutes we were ready to go. However, the police department needed to sign-off on the vehicle. There were people working in the police department section, but the person authorized to sign us out was not available. We were not the only people at the border, and the line was starting to back up.

After some investigation, we were told the one authorized to sign us out was in another town and would be back shortly. So, what could we do, except wait? If he took too long to return, the Costa Rican side of the border would close, and we would be stuck. Approximately an hour later, he arrived and signed-off on all the cars with no inspection; nothing more than a quick signature and we were ready to go. Now one wonders; just exactly where had the authorized police officer been? What was the big emergency that only he could handle? The reality was; he had been at a bar drinking and had come back to work at the end of the day to sign us out.

I finish my meeting with the pastors and inform them I will have to bring my time with them to an end as I am meeting with the teachers, and they are already waiting for me. The pastors inform me they will all be a part of that meeting too. I knew it was going to be a great time!

I walk in and notice immediately how nicely the room is set up. Everyone has arrived, and they are waiting on me. I take a few minutes to find out who is there and where they are from; learning about their ministry responsibilities before I begin teaching. This is a group of people who desire to be used by the Lord to teach others His Word. It is a privilege to be in such a beautiful place with these teachers. As we spend time studying the Word of God, I am pleased to learn how passionate this group of teachers and pastors is about learning and teaching. I am impressed by the questions they ask. They demonstrate a true desire to serve God. We end our meeting together in a time of prayer.

  It is now time for me to take my luggage, which I packed earlier, out of the room and head for the airport. Both M.L. and I will head to the airport, but we will be taking separate flights. M.L. will go back to Cali for a few days to see her family and then back home to Bogota. She has been a tremendous help, but I will complete the trip alone. Finishing alone was not a problem; especially since everything is ready and waiting for me to arrive in Medellin. M.L. hands me an envelope from a pastor in Cali. I open my carry-on luggage and put it in a pocket for safe keeping. I thank M.L. for all of her support. It has been a fantastic trip, and she is the one who helped organize all the events and set things in motion in Colombia. I wish her well and tell her to enjoy her family in Cali. We will be in touch via telephone once she returns to Bogota, and I am back in San Jose.

  I have just one more domestic/regional flight to take this afternoon. The flight from (PEI) Pereira to (EOH) Medellin is my last opportunity to fly in a small aircraft on this trip. I anticipate a remarkable flight traveling over, around and through the Andes Mountains. It is an awesome experience! The first time I traveled *over* the Andes was in a bus; both interesting and exciting! There was something new to see around every turn. It was gorgeous! These beautiful bus rides from Cali to Bogota can take ten to fourteen hours!

I remember the graduation trip with Paul and Donna Long. They had been to Costa Rica a few times and had heard about the work in Colombia. When the opportunity came to participate in the work of the ministry in Colombia by helping with graduations, they were ready and willing to go. There were several churches located along the mountainous road between Cali and Bogota whose students were ready to graduate. It was a difficult trip as we went from one town to another, going up and over the mountain range. Although the trip was not easy, it was quite picturesque, and the company of the travelers was excellent. Each church had a remarkable service for their graduates, as well as a noteworthy meal to honor their people.

I remember some places had their local version of 'arepas' and one congregation cooked a pig underground. I know it sounds strange, but it is a proven method to roast a pig. First, a hole is dug in the ground. Next, a fire is built in the hole. They then place the pig in the hole on top of the hot coals. The final step is to bury the hog.

These celebrations are always quite memorable for everyone involved. Paul and Donna did an incredible job, and their participation made it a pleasurable time. They have returned many times since then.

A word from
Paul and Donna Long

In 2003, my wife and I were pastoring and were invited to the January conference of Mutual Faith International in Mission Hills, California. During the day, several of the men were going golfing, but I had not made plans to go, so my wife and I decided to go to the John Paul Getty Museum. We learned that Don Korach was not golfing either, so Don joined us that afternoon. This was our first meeting with Don, and we spent the afternoon getting to know him and learning about his work in Latin America. I mentioned to him that I had done a Latin American missions trip with my father-in-law many years ago, and I have always wanted to start doing some short-term mission trips. Don invited my wife and me to come to Costa Rica. That spring we did, and that was the beginning of a wonderful friendship with Don and his family. It was also the beginning of several short-term mission trips.

It is awesome working with Don. Before we ever get there, he has our itinerary sent to us so we can plan accordingly. We are amazed at how organized and orderly things are when working with Don. His work in Costa Rica, actually all of Latin America, with the Bible Institute is absolutely amazing! We especially remember a trip where we traveled through Colombia in a VW bus over the Andes Mountains to participate in Bible Institute graduations.

One thing has remained in my memory about our first morning in Costa Rica. My wife and I had wanted to bring a gift for Rachel and Donnie. I think Rachel was nine, and Donnie was five. The gift we brought Donnie was a race car track similar to Hot Wheels, and the track had to be put together. There seemed to be a million pieces. The next morning, I got up early, and wouldn't you know it, so did Donnie! Guess what he wanted! Yes, to put the track together! That was the last time we ever bought a child a toy that needed to be assembled. It did make a wonderful memory for us ,though, and the Korach family has become one of our favorite families.

We are thankful to Don for getting us started in missions. After almost seventeen years of pastoring at our third church, we have taken the plunge into full-time missions!

Thank you, Don!

Paul and Donna Long
Paul Long Ministries
Apple Valley, CA

My travel, today, will be quick as we fly over the mountain range in the small plane. The aircraft will not be flying at an extremely high altitude, which means the view will be incredible. One such view is a snowcapped mountain. Only a few minutes into the flight there appears an enormous, majestic mountain reaching up into the sky with its beautiful year round snowcap. It is almost like a magical illusion. We fly through the white clouds and are suddenly surprised to see that the sun has a companion—this beautiful snowcapped mountain! There are so many breathtaking views to enjoy, but in what seems only minutes, we are descending to land in Medellin. The city of Medellin has two airports; the International Airport in Black River that is almost an hour from downtown and the old airport for commuter and light planes. We land at the (EOH) Medellin airport right in the heart of the city.

Once I arrive at the hotel and get checked in, there is something I want to do. The schedule has left me with a little down time, and I plan to use my time wisely. I do not have any meetings until the following day. Medellin has an above ground metro system similar to Chicago's *'L line'* (short for elevated). It is not an underground train like New York's subway system. The city of Medellin has completed a new branch called *'Metro Cable.'* The Metro Cable is a cable system that takes people straight up the mountainside. There is a station located only a block from the hotel. It is easy to access and quite secure, so I head for the station. Once I arrive at the station, I ask a police officer for help with a map. He is quick to assist me and point me in the right direction. The metro cars are crammed full of people. I begin to wonder if taking a ride today is such a good idea after all.

After stopping at a few stations, the crowd thins, and there is plenty of space for the remaining passengers and myself. Everyone seemed to get off at the *'stadium'* station. There is an important soccer game scheduled for this evening, and I can see that the local team will have lots of support from the fans.

In just a few minutes, I arrive at the new cable station. The station, along with the entire system, is notably clean. It is easy to see this means a great deal to the residents who take pride in their city. No one is eating, much less throwing trash on the floor; nor is there any graffiti painted on anything. Everyone made sure everything remained clean.

Getting on a metro (passenger train) is one thing, but getting on a cable car is a little strange at first. I notice the cable cars do not come to a full stop. As the cable cars, which only hold eight people, make the turn, you just walk with it and walk on. It sounds confusing because it is, but I just follow the crowd and let them show me how to get on. Once the cable car is out of the building, it speeds up and rushes up the mountain. It is easy to spot the tourists on the ride because when it feels like the car just drops down on the cable and whisks everyone away, all the tourists exclaim, "Ohhh!" Honestly, the residents seem a bit unimpressed with the whole process.

The ride up the mountain is impressive as I look out the window and see the lights over the city. The metro continues its journey up the mountain, slowing down so that people can get on or off at the various stations along the way.

As we go straight up, I can see vehicles seemingly crawling up the mountain on the winding roads. This new cable system goes up the mountain and dips down on the other side into a little valley filled with homes. As we dip down, the lights of the city of Medellin disappear, and it feels like we are in a different town. This happens twice on this route as the cars dip into tiny secluded places. The pastor I will be with on Sunday has an outreach for children at the location of the second dip. He and his team bring food and minister to them a couple times a week.

While walking back to the hotel, I begin to think about my schedule for the remainder of this trip. I have one more meeting with teachers and one more graduation. It has been a busy and productive time of ministry. I am so grateful I did not have to deal with dogs or dog bites on this trip.

The charter class in Nicaragua was holding its graduation that morning. Dr. Thompson sent a representative to help with the graduation, and Nago Piedra traveled with me from Costa Rica.

I had spent time the night before going through all the student files to ensure all was in order. We were staying in a small guest room at the pastor's compound. I was the first one up and ready, so I went to the pastor's home to see if there was anything we needed to do before the service.

As I walked out, Nago suggested I stay since there were dogs out in the yard. I told him I was aware of the dogs and that the pastor had already tied them up. He looked out the door to see if this was true since he had always been afraid of dogs. I, on the other hand, have never been afraid of them. Five steps out of the guest room, I walked past a big old Doberman. She is chained to a big tree, and so, I don't give her another thought; until I take my next step, and she leaps toward me. She broke the chain as though it was made from aluminum foil and then bit into my leg, ripping my pant leg to pieces!

With the commotion outside, the guys opened the door but would not come out of the guest room. They left me alone to fend for myself; alone in the yard with a crazy dog! This incident not only upset the guys in the guest room but also roused everyone in the compound! Before I knew it, the pastor arrived and dragged the dog away.

I was so upset that when the pastor asked me if I was ok I said, "Sure, but I need a shovel."

"A shovel? Why do you need a shovel?" He asked.

I then said, "Listen, pastor, do you like your kids?"

"Of course," he replied.

Still upset, I said to him, "Well if that dog is stupid enough to bite me, she could hurt or even kill one of your children! Bring me a shovel to bury the dog!"

Once I cleaned up, we held the graduation and all went well. Of course, I suddenly had a new nickname. The guys started calling me Alpo (aka dog food).

Once back at the hotel, I am ready to get something to eat and rest. I order a hamburger, fries, and a coke from room service and call it a day.

Day 12

I am in Town Looking for an Anchor

It is magnificent to begin the day in the city of Medellin. This is the last place of ministry before returning home. We have a large group of pastors and teachers scheduled for the day's teaching session, and the last graduation will be tomorrow.

The history of Medellin is an interesting one. It reaches back to 1616 where it was established by the Spaniards. In 1826, it was proclaimed the provincial capital of Antioquia. Way back in 1803, Antioquia founded a prestigious university, and that spirit of education is prevalent still today, with over thirty universities calling Medellin home. After Colombia won independence from Spain, Medellin became the capital of the Federal State of Antioquia. This independent state was short-lived and before the end of the century Medellin and Antioquia were once again part of Colombia. Medellin is in the Aburrá Valley, one of the northernmost valleys of the Andes Mountains in South America. It is the northern point of the Medellin, Cali, Bogota triangle.

Medellin was the first Colombian center to begin an 'industrial revolution.' Working in textiles and on transportation projects such as trains, made it possible to import and export. Coffee became a cash crop. It was one of the main products exported. The industrial and commercial attitude of Medellin has created a society of traders and entrepreneurs, which continues to impact the entire nation of Colombia and beyond.

In Medellin's more recent past, it is most famously touted as the home of Pablo Escobar and his infamous drug cartel. I can introduce you to countless pastors and ministers who worked for Escobar in the 1980's. Most of them went to prison and while in prison found Christ. When released, they never looked backed. They have continued to live faithfully and serve in the Kingdom of God.

Medellin's specific street design and functionality help traffic flow smoothly. Let me explain. In Bogota, there has been a huge effort to improve transportation. These efforts have helped, but traffic is miserably slow. Even in smaller San Jose, where I live, there is no particular plan or design in the layout of the city. People are offended when I tell them it looks as though cows designed San Jose, but this is not so far from the truth. If you knew the history of some of the streets and roads, you would agree. First, there was a cow path. Then, the path became a little larger, becoming a dirt road. Eventually, someone decided to lay asphalt on the dirt road. So, who might be considered the 'real' engineers to the road system? Cows! However, in Medellin, it is obvious that 'cows' did not design the roadways.

In my research, I discovered the 'Medellin Master Plan.' It was an architectural plan developed in the 1950's. It detailed the canalization of the Medellin River and the creation of residential, industrial, and even sports zones. Of course, it was not completed all at once, but at least there is a plan, and today, over fifty years later, Medellin is a comfortable, orderly city in which to live. The massive urban transportation service I had the privilege to enjoy, the Metro of Medellin, is a continuation of the ongoing development rooted in the Medellin Master Plan of the 1950's.

Medellin's climate seems quite similar to that of San Jose, Costa Rica. San Jose is about 4,000 feet above sea level. It is also located in a valley but a much larger valley then Medellin's Aburrá Valley. The altitude in Medellin is around five thousand feet above sea level. The average annual temperature of the city is a wonderful 72 degrees Fahrenheit. It is this pleasant climate that inspired one of a few nicknames for Medellin; City of the Eternal Spring. Other nicknames are *'Mountain Capital,' 'City of Flowers,' 'Orchids' Capital,' 'Beautiful Village,' 'Little Silver Cup,'* and *'Medallo,'* which is an endearing way to say Medellin.

We will not meet at the hotel where I am staying today. I must travel to another hotel only a couple of miles away to meet with the pastors and teachers. I am pleased that my driver is ready because I do not want to be late. I hope to have a bit of time to meet with the pastors before I teach. Although the streets are congested with traffic, especially in the downtown area, it will only take a few minutes to arrive at my destination. As we drive to the meeting, my phone rings.

"Hello, Keith! It is good to talk with you. Yes, only a couple more days in Colombia and I get to go home. Everything is going fantastic. The group did an incredible job, and I have had an excellent time alone as well. Ok, we will talk about the details of the next conference in a couple of days. Goodbye."

A word from Keith Hershey

As I hung up the phone from my conversation with Don about the scheduling of Bible Institute graduations in Latin America, I began to reminisce about the way we met so many years ago.

Don has worked in fellowship with me in Mutual Faith Ministries organization since 1991. His work throughout Central and South America has always blessed me immensely. He equips and trains thousands for leadership ministry in local churches.

Don and I first met in Tulsa, Oklahoma in 1982. We were both Bible school students, and both employed for a short season at the CITY OF FAITH. This was an enormous hospital structure that world famous healing evangelist Oral Roberts built to merge the ministries of prayer and medicine.

Don and I were hired to move the new furniture into the structure. There were three towers to this building. The tallest tower was sixty stories tall! Needless to say, there was a lot of furniture to move into that facility!

Don and I were paired up on many occasions, moving desks, credenzas, file cabinets and chairs throughout all the executive offices and secretarial stations.

It was during this time that I learned of Don's heart for the nations and his desire to serve the Lord as a missionary in the foreign field. We spent a great deal of time talking about ideas and methodology for evangelism and ministry! It is amazing to see how the Lord used that time and season to seal our hearts together and later allowed us to join our faith for mission opportunities throughout Central and South America.

I have always known Donald Korach to be a man of integrity and diligent in the work of the Kingdom of God. What a joy to see all God has done and continues to do – in his life and through his life, throughout this Latin American region!

Keith Hershey
President and Founder
Mutual Faith International

As Keith and I end our call, I make a note to call him when I return home. For a moment, I pondered how our International Conference attendance had increased from hundreds to thousands; all of this thanks to the conference in Panama.

Our meeting in Panama was with one of the associate pastors with Hosanna. We meet up with Pastor A.O. for breakfast at a Chinese restaurant. I know it sounds odd to go to a Chinese restaurant for breakfast, but the Chinese prepare a delicious morning meal! The menu consists of tea accompanied by dumplings, filled buns, vegetables, desserts and fruit. At first it may seem a bit unconventional, but that is only the case if you

have never had the privilege of eating dim sum in Panama City, Panama!

I began by greeting the Pastor. "It is great to see you again, Pastor! Thanks for coming!" At the same time, men pushing carts began delivering food to tables. We chose a few items that looked enticing. Once we had briefly engaged in a bit of small talk, Pastor Ortiz asked me what I was doing in Panama and how he could help. I did not want to say, "Pastor. We want to hold a conference in Panama, and we want to use your church!" I simply said, "Pastor, I am in town looking for an anchor."

Growing up in Minnesota, I had neighbors who lived across the lake; Marty and Dee Martinson. Mr. Martinson was an engineer/designer of shopping malls. Please take note that when you live on a lakeside, you have neighbors that you can visit either by boat or by making the drive in a vehicle. Driving around the lake is always an option, but a true lake neighbor is someone you visit via the water.

On one occasion, when Mr. Marty Martinson and I were visiting and just talking shop, he told me he was in the middle of a big project. I suppose anytime you build a mall it is a 'big' project, but what I found interesting was that he used the term 'anchor.' Thankfully, he took the time to explain what he meant when referring to the three anchors of this particular project. The only anchor I had ever seen was one tied to a boat. He explained that every mall must have 'anchors' in order to bring in shoppers. For example, if a mall is made up of only small stores, the project will fail. The larger the anchor, the better, and the more anchors available, the better! When people go to the larger stores, or 'anchor' stores in a mall, they will often patronize the smaller specialty stores as well.

Immediately Pastor Ortiz understood what I was looking for; I wasn't interested in just planning another activity. I was looking for a church willing to work together with us, whereby both ministries would complement one another. I wasn't looking for something to do for a weekend. My goal was to find someone with whom to develop a relationship in order to continue working together in the future.

The word picture was highly effective as it only took one small word, 'anchor,' for us to completely understand each other. With this simple word, we had an understanding. All his life Pastor had observed boats and ships anchored out in front of the Panama Canal waiting their turn to pass through the canal.

His immediate question was, "Is your boat big enough to handle our anchor?" This was a very good question!

My response? "Yes, our ship is large enough!"

It was there, in the middle of this seemingly odd breakfast venue, surrounded by statues of Buddha and carvings of dragons on the ceiling, that a vital new relationship was born. Within a couple of days, he had spoken with the senior pastor about the vision. We spent the next few months preparing for our largest conference ever, and we quickly progressed from hundreds to thousands of attendees! We also went from printing posters to promote the conference to advertising on television. Panama was the pivot point that changed the way we handled our international conference going forward. I mentioned to Elmer Flores during our drive back to Costa Rica that working in Panama could possibly change the ministry forever. I believe it has done just that!

I arrive at the hotel feeling like I am entering the building through the back door. It may be because I am entering through the parking lot and not the street entrance. I want to check my email before going upstairs, but the business service center is not yet open. It only takes a moment, and a staff member directs me to a cubicle where I have access to a computer. I check my e-mail and find news from Marjorie informing me that all is well on the home front. She also wants to confirm my arrival time for the trip back home. The e-mail from home tugs on my heart, and for a moment, I long to be back home. I quickly refocus and continue with my mission on this trip.

I remember when Donnie was just a little guy. One day he thought playing with a wallet filled with money might be a fun thing to do. I don't know about you, but I have extensive experience in losing things such as keys, wallets, etc. In fact, I have misplaced a few wallets in my day.

One day I had exchanged some money into local currency. This meant I had a wallet full of cash that needed to be taken to the bank. I soon realized the wallet was not where it was supposed to be; it was gone. Had I left it at the money exchange office, at the ministry office? Was it in the car? I had no idea! Marjorie began the search at home, and I went to the ministry office to see if I could locate the missing wallet. When I arrived at the office, Marjorie was calling me to inform me of the good news; she had found my wallet with all the money still inside! She found it on the front seat of one of Donnie's toy cars.

On another occasion, Donnie grabbed the moneybag. I had not put the cash in my wallet. He grabbed the bag filled with money and went outside. I went out after him, but he had an obvious head start, and he headed straight for the gate! Our home is enclosed by a concrete wall with a gate that goes out into the street. Donnie ran to the gate, pulled the money from the bag and threw it through the gate onto the street! At that moment, all of our money began blowing down the sidewalk toward the neighbor's gate. I found myself standing there facing a locked gate with no key in hand! Donnie was standing next to me with an empty moneybag. I had no other choice but to yell out to Marjorie to push the button for the gate to open automatically. In just a second or two, I was outside the gate working quickly to gather the money. Marjorie came out wondering what all the commotion was about while Donnie stood there laughing. He very much enjoyed the drama! When I think about the incident today, it makes me laugh as well though it was anything but funny at the time!

I take the stairs to the second-floor meeting area, and I am greeted by the group of pastors. I met most of the pastors who are utilizing the Bible Institute in Medellin approximately two years ago in Bogota, and some of these pastors will be graduating tomorrow evening.

Medellin is the city where I had hoped ministry in Colombia would have its beginning. However, the Lord directed us to other cities first. It is now Medellin's turn, and though we already have some students here, this is a time for the pastors and myself to establish closer relationships. It is an exciting time for us all, as this is our first main activity together!

My teaching time with the pastors and teachers is productive, and fellowship during breaks and lunch is beneficial in establishing relationships. They are here with positive attitudes and open hearts to learn the role of a teacher and what the Bible says about them. It is truly a joy to be with such dedicated people!

One of the Pastors invites me to minister at his church later this evening. I tell him it would be my pleasure! He arranges my transportation to the church and tells me to be ready by 5:00 p.m. The service is scheduled for 6:00 p.m., but it will take about forty-five minutes to get to the church on that side of town.

When you talk to others about Medellin, they always say the same thing; it is an attractive city, but it has a closed culture. The only thing the people from Medellin are interested in is doing business with you. Loosely translated - they want to take your money. This, however, has not been my experience in Medellin. It is a beautiful city, and everywhere I go I find I am with the very best people; members of the Body of Christ. I can see that it may very well seem to be a closed culture since you are either on the inside looking out, on the outside looking in, or completely out! Still I maintain; I have not had this experience. I find the people of Medellin to be some of the friendliest, most hospitable people I have ever met. They open their home, ministries and lives to me. While with them, I have never felt I was on the outside looking in. The love and power of God flow through each member as the body supplies every need! This power is much more compelling than any culture in the world!

This is my last night in Colombia for this trip. I will be busy right up to the last minute due to the previously unscheduled invitation to minister in the service at Pastor Blass' church. There will be no time for *'not one step back mode'* thinking today. There is one last graduation service tomorrow morning and a flight home later in the day. Everything is in order, and I am so grateful for the many accomplishments of recent days.

The driver from Pastor Blass' church arrives right on time. I am prepared for the long ride to the other side of town. Additionally, I am thankful for the nice hotel I will be staying in tonight as hotel stays are not always a pleasant experience.

On our first trip to Colombia, I came with Dillious and Bonnie Bowman. We all flew into Cali. From there, we went by land to Armenia. It was an enjoyable and productive time there, but our Armenian friends knew nothing about Cali, and we knew even less! We made the drive from Armenia to Cali, and it was late at night when we arrived at the hotel. The hotel we were supposed to stay at in Cali turned out to be a terrible place; noticeable even in the darkness of night! I did not like it, and I especially did not like it for my guests. I remembered that there were a few rooms at the airport; so we drove all the way back to the airport and slept there for the night. Dillious and Bonnie Bowman have always been very kind and patient. After all, it was our first trip to Cali, and the airport worked out just fine. Since then, I have found excellent hotels in Cali and for that I am most grateful!

It takes exactly forty-five minutes to arrive at our destination. The next thing I see touches my heart deeply. In fact, Pastor Blass will always have a special place in my heart. The driver pulls up to a home that looks like most homes in the area. It is a two-story home with a garage and kitchen on the first floor and bedrooms located on the second floor. Pastor Blass had turned his home into a church! The garage is now a sanctuary, and the kitchen looks like community property as ladies from the church are busy preparing food. They want to make sure the pastor and I have a hot meal after the service. How very kind of them.

Pastor Blass and I have had many meals at his home since. The food is wonderful, but the best part, as far as I am concerned, is the time we spend sharing. I have learned about Medellin and how it used to be years ago. I have learned how the Lord changed their lives and called them into the ministry.

Pastor Blass has a strong Medellinian accent; unique and interesting. Anyone familiar with this accent would immediately recognize that Pastor Blass had grown up in Medellin and subsequently lived there his entire life!

You are doing something at this moment that Pastor Blass could never do when he was young. When he was a child, he never learned to read. Life was too difficult to allow time for schooling. If he needed to know something he would ask Lilian, his wife, to read it to him. When they were called to the ministry, his prayer was, "Lord, I cannot be a Pastor if I can't read the Bible." Amazingly, from that day on he could, would and does read the Bible! However, if you asked him to read the newspaper he cannot and would still have Lillian do it for him.

After my initial visit to the church, there would be graduations to celebrate and more times of teaching to this congregation. If I was ever in Medellin, I always found a reason to see them. They were always kind and caring, and though they were an older couple when I met them, they were young at heart; full of vision and hope for the future. They embraced the Bible Institute and used it to train and transform their congregation. The last time I was with Pastor Blass and Lillian the Lord had blessed them with additional finances, and he was doing a major remodeling of the church. They were building classrooms for the children and fixing up the little apartment for them and their little dog. A few months after finishing this major building project, Pastor Blass went home to be with the Lord. His love and his life will impact my life forever.

As I ride up in the hotel elevator to my room, I thank God for my time in Medellin and for such great friends in such an incredible city!

Day 13

"Graduation Bonanza!" Comes to a Close But it is Just the Beginning!

Last night, a package arrived for me. It was a huge box containing some of the files for the graduates. I need to get all this information back to Costa Rica. Mr. Chaves, one of the young men here at the hotel, helps me get everything weighed and packed, so that when I get to the airport I won't have any surprises waiting for me regarding overweight bags.

Breakfast at the hotel is nice, and the service is wonderful. As I finish up my coffee, I remember the very first beginnings of the Bible Institute.

I was in the United States, in the state of Missouri visiting churches and keeping them abreast of what was happening in the ministry. On this trip, I stayed at the home of Pastor David Craig in Sikeston, Missouri. Pastor Craig had often talked to me about a bible college with which he was affiliated. I must admit; I had never given it much thought, but on this particular day, we had some free time, so I went to their church and previewed some of the material and files from the bible college. It was during that visit and those couple of hours that I fell in love with the material and immediately inquired how I might obtain this tool and get it into the hands of pastors for use in training their people.

I immediately made a phone call over to the state of Illinois and spoke with the president of the International Institute of Bible Theology, Dr. Verda Thompson. She agreed to let us use the materials. Within a couple of days, she began sending material over to Missouri for me to take back to Costa Rica. To get this material into the hands of students, it must be translated from English into Spanish.

Dr. Thompson and I communicated via fax and telephone working out the details. It was two years before Dr. Thompson and I met in person, but through this connection, this small bible college continues to touch lives around the world.

The first classes of the Bible Institute were taught in Tres Rios, Costa Rica, approximately twenty minutes from San Jose. I made contact with Dr. Thompson in the fall of 1996, and on the first Monday of March 1997 we held our first classes. We had translated enough material by then to begin the first trimester of classes. That first group of students kept us very busy. It became quite normal for us to translate the material, place it immediately into the hands of the students, and continue translating questions not yet prepared for use.

Dr. Thompson was kind enough to send a representative, Pastor Gary Manning to help get us started. Pastor Gary Manning pointed us in the right direction and helped us tremendously. Though we do not always do this, in Tres Rios we decided to have two groups of students, a Monday group, and a Friday group. When I printed the materials for these initial classes, it was a guess as to how much we needed to have printed. I am a man of faith, so I decided on fifty copies to start. My thinking? How wonderful it would be to have twenty-five students on Monday and another group of twenty-five on Friday. As God would have it, we ran out of material the first day of orientation and had to have more printed for the Friday group. In all, we began with a total of eighty-five students!

Originally, my desire was to help out this one local pastor, but it wasn't long before another pastor wanted the materials in his church and then another and another.

The first country in which the Bible Institute was exported outside of Costa Rica was to Colombia. There was a young man from Colombia, who was a part of the church in Tres Rios. He had lived in Costa Rica for a couple of years but felt it was time to go back home and start a church. His desire was to take the Bible Institute back with him. We were happy to help him get started.

A word from
Gary Manning
Ministry Trip to Costa Rica with Donald Korach

This trip to Costa Rica with Donald came some eight years after I had left Costa Rica as a resident missionary to that country. I had met Donald for the first time in Missouri where I was speaking at a mission conference for a local Bible Institute. After spending some time with Donald and talking about missions, he invited me to visit Costa Rica again. What a great encounter that turned out to be! On this trip, Donald and I crossed the low hills of Costa Rica's mountain range and then dipped down to the Pacific side of that tiny nation. We arrived at the city of Puntarenas, the capital and largest city in the Province of Puntarenas. The meeting Donald had scheduled was held under a metal roof in the open air. It was sweltering and muggy. Nonetheless, it was exciting to see a group of twenty plus local church leaders gather to hear about the new pastoral leadership ministry program. It has been a great pleasure and honor to watch Donald achieve his long-desired goal of bringing much needed training to pastors and leaders in places like Puntarenas throughout Costa Rica. It was here that I witnessed the heart and vision of Donald and the school in a very real way. His diligence and hard work have achieved more than I could have ever expected. I remain grateful that he allows me to remain a small part of this great ministry.

Ministry Trip to Cali, Colombia

Years went by after that first trip to Costa Rica. Then, Donald invited me to travel with him to Cali, Colombia in South America. I had never visited Colombia, and I was very excited at the opportunity. Even more than visiting a new country, I was excited to see how God was using Donald to take the ministry he had built in Costa Rica into yet another country. When we arrived in Cali, we spent the next five days ministering to church leaders in that city. We discussed with the leaders, the school we would bring to them. Eventually, this school would touch and train more than 3,000 students of God's word to prepare them for ministry in their local churches. The reception of these leaders was overwhelming. While Cali is a beautiful city geographically, it is riveted with problems...from drug lords to violent thieves roaming the streets of the city. While staying in Cali, we were warned against traveling outside of the city because kidnapping of foreigners was prevalent by certain anti-government groups. However, Donald and I were not deterred by the problems of the city. After all, what better place to equip God's people? As Scripture teaches, where sin abounds, grace much more abounds!

**Pastor Gary Manning,
North Carolina**

Yesterday, I asked Pastor Fernando Colorado if he could pick me up a little early, so we might have a few minutes together before going to service. He, of course, obliges. As I finish checking out of the hotel, Pastor Fernando pulls up, but he is alone.

"I expected to see your family. Where are they?" I asked.

"Well, I knew you would have your luggage, so I have already taken them to the church to give us plenty of room," he replied.

I ask Mr. Chaves to watch my bags for a moment, and Pastor Fernando and I take a quick walk over to the Botero Square in front of the hotel. The park is filled with many bronze statues made by native-born Fernando Botero. He is a famous painter and sculptor who creates obese subjects. His work can be found in various places around the world. After a few pictures and laughs, we know we must head toward the church. "Pastor Fernando, it is a good thing you didn't bring your family because your car is filled with my luggage!"

As we pull up to the church, two young men come to help us carry the luggage inside. Stepping into the building, I see a staircase leading to the sanctuary. Pastor Fernando is excited about being in this new location. It is larger than where they were located before and is less expensive. There is only one drawback; it is on the second floor.

Pastor Fernando's wife is practicing with the singers. The young drummer who looks like he is having a magnificent time is their youngest son. A young man in the church comes up and admires the video camera. After a quick lesson, I now have a video and still shot photographer. As the graduates arrive, they dress in their graduation robes. I make sure to gather all their signatures before the service. The pastor's wife says she will finish gathering the signatures for me. The pastor had the robes made for his graduates, and they look great!

I find a seat over on the left side and wait for the service to begin. Both the pastor and I are the last to put on our graduation clothes. He will graduate today as well!

The praise and worship is good, but it is the young drummer who impresses me the most. He plays those drums with every fiber of his being! When it came time to minister the

Word of God, the students are over to my right on a four-step balcony. In front of me is the main part of the sanctuary. It is filled with church members. As I make my way through the Word, I have a great time with the church as well as the graduates. I give my new photographer a workout as I wander around the church while ministering.

As we hand out the diplomas, the entire church applauds and cheers for each graduate. When their pastor receives his diploma, the church gives him a standing ovation! One, two, three, and the caps go into the air! The graduates are excited, and the congregation is proud! As the hats are picked up off the floor, *"Graduation Bonanza!"* comes to a close. When we finish, I realize I went longer than intended. As soon as Pastor Fernando closes the service, we need to be on our way. I have one more plane to catch, and this one is headed home.

On the way to the (MDE) Medellin International Airport, I ask the pastor about his drummer. I wonder if he has taken any lessons. He replied, "My son said to me one day that he wanted to play drums for the church, but we didn't have any drums. So, once we had enough money, I asked him if he really wanted to play drums for the church as he had said, and he assured me that he did. He is self-taught and has been playing since then. He is the first to arrive at practice and the last to leave."

I said, "Of course he is! You bring him and take him home!" We both enjoy a laugh as we travel along the road.

Making our way toward the airport, I ask him if he has ever been to the airport. He tells me he has not. I am thinking, no problem, there will be many signs, right? Well, after driving for quite a while, we begin to feel lost. You know that feeling you get; have I gone too far or not far enough? With two men in the car, there is no one to ask for directions, but eventually we are forced to do so. We have gone too far and somehow missed the turn, but no harm is done. We have only gone a couple of miles out of the way. Once we find the correct turnoff, the signs guide us the rest of the way to the airport.

At the airport, I have to get some help. I have too many bags now because of the student files. Pastor Fernando and I shake hands at the curb. He thanks me one more time for the graduation of his people today. I remind him the pleasure was all mine. As he drives off, the gentleman with the cart holding my luggage leads me into the airport to the correct counter. As we are walking, I tap my blazer pocket, and I am thankful everything seems to be in order.

Just a few months ago, I was flying out of San Jose. I did all the counter stuff to check in, and a gentleman with the airline went in the back with my passport and didn't come back for twenty minutes. He came back and said to me "Mr. Korach we need your paper ticket."

I said, "What paper ticket this is an e-ticket. Let me see what I can do."

"Well, no. It's not, and I can't get you on the flight without the paper."

"Let me see what I can do," I called the travel agent's office upset about the ticket trouble. She called me back and said, "Don, you signed for the ticket on such and such date, you have the ticket. Let me see what I can do."

Then I called Marjorie and asked her to check the safe, which I know has no ticket in it, and she says, "This ticket? Yes, it's here."

Oh no! What can I do?! I don't have the time to go back home and catch the flight. I call the office and tell Elmer to go to my house, pick up the ticket, take my car and get here as fast as you can. I have forty-five minutes to one hour max, or I won't be flying today!

I talked with the travel agent again. She tells that she is working to get me on the flight. She tells me the flight is full, and so are the flights for the next four days. She tells me to give my bags to the airlines; they will hold the bags and my seat up to the last minute.

Elmer arrives at the airport forty minutes from the call. He doesn't even get out of the car. He pulls up to the curb passes the ticket to me through the window, and I walk back into the terminal. I give the people at the counter the paper ticket, and I run to the gate. There won't be any coffee today. I get to the gate to find that there has been a gate change. When I get to the alternate gate, the airline workers are surprised to see me and congratulate me on my arrival. I just walk right on the plane, and it isn't until then that I look at my seat assignment. The airline had given me an upgrade. So, even though I had messed up, they blessed me with a row three seat.

I get all the luggage checked in and head for security with my boarding pass. I know there is no restaurant or anything after security, so I take a quick detour for a cup of coffee. There is plenty of time. There shouldn't be any problems. When I sit down for a cup of coffee and look at my carry on, I remember the envelope ML gave me. The pastor from Cali had very kindly written the following.

Refreshment in Tough Times

Colombia is one of the most beautiful countries in Latin America, but like a girl that prostitutes herself without thinking about the risks, it was hit by corruption and death.

In 1999, its citizens were going through one of the worst storms of violence. Drug dealing became more powerful; the guerrilla was unleashed, and violence was present in most families. We, as church leaders, were going through a time when we needed people to remain steady in the Lord. We needed people to learn about God's Word and reap blessings because these tough moments would only allow those who were prepared and disciplined to survive. During this time of chaos in our country, especially in the city of Cali, Donald Korach helped us.

I met Donald in the year 2000 when he knocked on our church's door and introduced his Bible Institute to us. That's where a bond, not only professional but a bond of friendship began. He gave us the tools to start the preparation and shaping of our members. He supported us during the whole process, even if our city was being attacked by car bombs, hit men, and death at all times.

At my church, we considered Donald's arrival as an answer to our prayers. We had tried to grow and learn with other institutes, but they all had something that never allowed us to finish their programs, either money, time, etc. Finally, the answer we were waiting for; God, who never forgot us, heard our prayers and delivered through Don's hands. He gave us a tool to help not only our congregation but also Colombia. I have met many people from churches in distant locations within our country thanks to the Ministry Don introduced us to.

He not only introduced us to the Institute, but he also took the risk of visiting us periodically. He still visits us and has gone to places that very few have dared to visit! He took the risk of visiting a country in chaos, and this motivation lead him to my church and many others. Today, his spirit is still as dauntless as before, visiting extremely dangerous places in our country.

We will never deny that God helped and blessed Colombia, and is still blessing it, with Don's Bible Institute and his dedication to us. My country has been fertilized with words of wisdom from Donald and his Ministry. I could continue telling stories about the adventures and risks Donald took for us and all the forgotten places that were blessed by him. If I could describe what Donald Korach means for us in five words, I would say he is 'A Refreshment in Tough Times.'

Pastor R.M.
Pastor in Cali

Once through passport control and security all I have to do is find the gate. Upon finding the gate, security looks at my passport one last time and asks to go through my luggage *again*. I think to myself, you all really *don't* trust each other do you? However, I am mistaken. They don't want to look through my carry on. They want to look through my checked bags that they have brought to the gate instead of the plane. So, as I watch, they go through my luggage. They obviously could have done this without me, but they wanted me present. After all the flights I have been on the last few days, now, when it is time to leave, they want to demonstrate their authority! It is only a few minutes of inconvenience, and I choose not to think any more of it.

Now that my ministry assignments for this trip are finished here in Colombia, I can't stop thinking about what awaits me back home. I get to be with my family again, which is great. In a couple of weeks, there will be another ministry team visiting from the United States to minister in Costa Rica. They won't be a part of *"Graduation Bonanza!"* or any graduation; there will be other expressions of ministry. There are classes to be taught and ministry to orphans and the elderly. It will be a great rounded trip, with some tourism mixed with ministry. We won't be building churches, but it will be good. When I think of the coming group, I am reminded of the groups from Trinity Assembly and how they have helped over the years.

I received a call from Dillious and Bonnie Bowman one day, and they said the church was in a big building project, and they wanted to sow a seed of a church building on the mission field. I thought, Wow! What a great act of faith! After talking to various pastor friends of mine, we found the one that would work the best. We built this church way up in the mountains.

We talked with a Canadian company that was just beginning to build prefab custom buildings here in Costa Rica. I showed them the plans of the building. They said it could be done, and were excited about the challenge. They were anxious to say they could build a church and not just homes. Before they would agree to the contract, they needed to send their representative to the lot of the future building site to see if it was possible. He checked it out, and in about a week I was signing a contract for the building.

It took them about a month to get all the pieces made, which I needed to have in place, and all put together before the group from Trinity arrived to complete the building.

Three weeks before the group was to arrive, and a day before the big day, I received a call from the Canadian Construction Company. It was a short call. "Don, we have a problem. We need you here at our office as soon as you can get here." It took a few hours, but I did get there as fast as possible.

"Don we have all the pieces of the church made and loaded on two semi-trucks ready to go to the building site, but we made a big mistake. Our representative went to the building site, but he must be blind. We can't get our trucks to the site. It is way up in the mountains, and we won't get past half of those tight turns up the mountain. Let us give you back your money, and you do something else.

I said, "Guys, I have a group that will be here in just a few days ready to finish the building. I can't just start a new project. There is no time. They thought about it and talked among themselves for a while, then said, "Don, we have an idea. We won't make any money on this project, but it was our fault, not yours. Tomorrow, we will send your building to the site.

The next day they brought the pieces not to the construction site but to the bottom of the mountain and unloaded them in a cow pasture. From there, they loaded one piece at a time onto a dump truck and piece-by-piece, truck-by-truck they took the building up the mountain to the building site.

The entire community up on the mountain and all the little communities along the way stopped what they were doing to see what was happening. The local school stopped classes so the students could watch a building be built in a day. People still talk about it. This was a big, big deal!

Trinity sent a group of nineteen people, and they finished the building. They would work by day and preach by night. The closest hotel for the group was an hour away, and each day they had to go up and down the mountain. The group informed me that there were ninety-nine curves going up the mountain.

The church helped, and the group worked hard. On the group's last day of their seven-day visit, pastors of the region and fellow Christians of the area came to be a part of the dedication. That church is the nicest in the area, and the people that congregate there touch lives every day with the gospel. Trinity has sent many groups over the years; some were youth, others adults. Over the years, Trinity has helped build three different churches here in Costa Rica!

A word from Pastor Mike Campbell

What a joy it was to be part of this building project! A member of our congregation began to tell us about a missionary in Costa Rica who was doing a good work and had a town that needed a church. It was a remote area of Costa Rica so we would have to stay in a coastal town called Puntarenas. Daily we traveled up the mountain to the town where we built the church. It was quite the crew who made this odyssey. It was our first church mission trip since I had joined the church staff, and it was the very first mission trip for my wife and me.

One thing I remember most was how Don and I drove the vehicles, and raced down the mountain. It was not the brightest thing I have ever done but caught up in the moment it was what we did. When I returned from the trip, this action earned me a time of correction from my Pastor. I was also grounded from driving church vehicles.

Each day we were in Costa Rica we worked hard to finish this project. We mixed and poured concrete. We wired, put in fixtures, roofed, built a sound booth, painted, and did some woodwork. We marveled at how some who helped us had walked many miles to be a part of what God was doing in this small town. It was a marvelous project for our first mission trip, and it brought a great sense of satisfaction. We had one man who disappeared when the work began. We later found him playing stickball with all the kids who had been watching the crew. We had two men who would go out into town in the evening to eat and see the town. Neither could speak the language, but both came back with their bellies full. When asked what they needed, they said they would point to their mouths and rub their stomachs. The place answered their request with a cheeseburger! Good communication skills always pay big dividends!

We enjoyed the experience with Don, and that led to other projects with him. He was always ready when we arrived and never got worked up when we requested things he could not produce from a local hardware store that was most certainly not Lowes or Home Depot!

We preached, we sang, we gave thanks, we built, and God brought increase in our lives. In the process, a church building was completed.

Many years ago, we thought we were only building a church, but since then, this trip to Costa Rica has remained in our hearts.

Pastor Mike Campbell
Trinity Assembly, Tennessee

In just a few minutes, my row is called. I settle into an aisle seat and think to myself... *the next words I want to hear are, "Welcome to San Jose!"*

About the Author

Dr. Donald Korach is affiliated with Mutual Faith, Mission Hills, CA and has labored in the foreign field for over thirty years. A missionary in Central and South America since 1984, Don is originally from the state of Minnesota, USA but currently lives in Costa Rica with his wife Marjorie and children Rachel and Donnie. Don is the director of the Costa Rica Mission and head of the International Institute of Bible Theology with thousands of graduates in several Latin American nations.

Don and Marjorie

Dr. Donald M. Korach, Missionary
(506) 88214944 cell/whatsapp
Email: dkorach@femutua.org

Fe Mutua - Mutual Faith Costa Rica
Phone: (506) 2235-7707
Apdo Postal: 1211-2150, Moravia, San José, Costa Rica.
Email: dkorach@mutualfaith.org
Website:www.femutua.org

Made in the USA
San Bernardino, CA
31 December 2016